WHAT'S COOKING

BURT WOLF

WHAT'S COOKING PRODUCTIONS, INC.
BOX 2000-ANSONIA STATION, NEW YORK, NY 10023

EXECUTIVE PRODUCER
EMILY ARONSON

ASSOCIATE PRODUCER
CAROLINE McCOOL

BOOK PRODUCTION
DANIEL KLAYMAN

TEST CHEFS
VINCENT BECKLEY
DEBORAH DARLINGTON
KATY KECK
MARY LYNN MONDICH

BOOK MANUFACTURER
S.C. TOOF & COMPANY
MEMPHIS, TENNESSEE

TABLE OF CONTENTS

POULTRY

MEATS

PASTA & RICE

VEGETABLES

DESSERTS, CAKES, TARTS, COOKIES & A PIE

BREADS, PIZZA, PANCAKES, MARMALADE, JAM, A SEASONING AND TWO BEVERAGES

FOLKLORE

INTRODUCTION

The research and videotapings that were used as the basis for this book took me to Oregon, Canada, Idaho, Puerto Rico, Norway, England and France. Among other things, Oregon showed us the seafood cookery that has been part of the history of northwestern cooking for thousands of years. Canada brought us to the kitchen of an old fort that was a center for fur trappers from 1803 to 1821 and across the provinces of Manitoba, Saskatchewan and Ontario. The potato harvest was the attraction in Idaho, as well as the state's extensive natural beauty. Puerto Rico was an island-wide visit with some of the great local cooks.

Norway harvested its 100 millionth farm-raised salmon, cooked their favorite salmon recipes, took us to the kitchen of a working farm that is precisely as it was in the late 1700's, and to the galley of the first explorer ship to reach the South Pole. Harrods Department store in London, lent us their food halls so we could talk about some of the traditional dishes of England. The Ritz Hotel in Paris and their cooking school helped tell the story of Cesar Ritz (the master of the great hotels of the late 1800's) and Auguste Escoffier (Ritz's chef) and their unbeatable recipes. Escoffier loved to invent dishes for famous friends. His gift to the singer Nellie Melba included Melba Toast and Peach Melba. We also cooked our way through the low-calorie menus at the Ritz Hotel Health Club.

My intention in this small book is to share with you some of the things I learned during this four-month trip. I hope you enjoy them as I did.

Burt Wolf

A Welsh Rarebit is never such a success
as when served with delicious

Gilt Edge Beer

This amber brew adds to an evening
lunch as "pepper to a curry."

The Minneapolis Brewing Co.

Beer Advertisement 1896

SOUPS & STEWS

NORWEGIAN SALMON SOUP
HOTEL NORGE ♦ BERGEN, NORWAY

For over 100 years, the Hotel Norge in Bergen has been a gastronomic landmark. The following salmon soup recipe was a gift from the hotel's chef.

2 tablespoons vegetable oil
1 carrot, cut into matchstick pieces
1 celery stalk, cut into matchstick pieces
3 red potatoes, cut into $1/2$-inch cubes
$1/2$ teaspoon garlic, minced
$1/2$ teaspoon thyme
1 quart clam juice
1 cup water
1 Bay leaf
2 tablespoons tomato puree
1 pound salmon, boned, skinned, and diced into bite sized pieces
$1/4$ cup chopped parsley
1 tablespoon capers
1 tablespoon gherkin pickles, chopped

1. Heat the oil in a large saute pan or stock pot. Add the vegetables, garlic and thyme and cook over medium heat for 5 minutes. Add clam juice, water and the Bay leaf and let the soup simmer for 15 minutes.

2. Add the tomato puree and salmon and simmer for 15 additional minutes. Add parsley, capers and gherkins. Remove and discard the Bay leaf.

Makes 4 servings

BLACK BEAN STEW
HEATHMAN HOTEL ♦ PORTLAND, OREGON

Scientists are telling us that the fiber and other nutrients found in beans and legumes can be more valuable to our body than those in oats. The information was taken to heart by Chef George Tate at the Heathman Hotel in Portland, Oregon, when he prepared the following recipe.

2 cups dried black beans
4 tablespoons olive oil, divided as follows
1/2 pound fully cooked lean peppered ham or Virginia style ham, cut into bite sized pieces
1/2 pound fully cooked sausage, cut into bite sized pieces
1/2 pound fully cooked lean roast beef, cut into bite sized pieces
3 cloves of garlic, minced
1 medium onion, chopped
1 tomato, chopped
3 cups prepared whole grain or Basmati rice

1. In a medium bowl, soak the beans overnight in 4 cups of cold water. Drain and rinse the beans.

2. In a medium saucepan, cook the beans in 4 cups of cold water until tender, about 2 1/2 hours. The beans should have some liquid remaining. If needed, add 1/2 to 1 cup water during the last half hour of cooking.

3. In a large skillet, heat 2 tablespoons of the oil. Add the cooked ham, sausage and beef and saute over medium heat until heated through, about 4 minutes.

4. In another large skillet, heat the remaining 2 tablespoons of oil. Add the garlic and onion and saute over medium heat for 3 minutes. Add the tomato and saute for 3 more minutes. Add the black beans. Cook until heated through, about 4 minutes.

5. Add the beans to the meat and heat through, about 4 minutes. Serve with rice and the following citrus salsa.

Makes 6 servings

CITRUS SALSA
HEATHMAN HOTEL ♦ PORTLAND, OREGON

1 red onion, chopped
1 red bell pepper, chopped, ribs and seeds discarded
1 medium cucumber, quartered lengthwise and sliced
2 oranges, peeled and chopped
1 small jalapeño, finely minced
2 tablespoons fresh parsley, chopped
3 tablespoons rice wine vinegar
3 tablespoons white wine vinegar
3 drops of Tabasco

1. In a medium bowl, combine the onion, pepper, cucumber, oranges and jalapeño.

2. In a small bowl, combine the parsley, both vinegars, and the Tabasco.

3. Toss the mixtures together and serve chilled.

Makes 6 cups

SPANISH LENTIL SOUP
AMADEUS RESTAURANT
OLD SAN JUAN, PUERTO RICO

West Africans were brought to Puerto Rico by Spanish colonists as the labor for the sugar cane plantations. Of the many elements that the West Africans brought to Puerto Rican cooking, two of my favorites are the use of lentils and the introduction of thick soups. For other recipes from the Amadeus Restaurant see pages 20, 21 and 120.

1 pound lentils
2 Bay leaves
2 sprigs parsley
$1/4$ pound bacon, cut into small cubes
3 tablespoons olive oil
3 medium onions, chopped
2 carrots, scraped and finely chopped
$1/2$ tablespoon chopped garlic
2 teaspoons paprika
Salt and freshly ground black pepper
$1/2$ pound spicy Italian sausage
3 tablespoons red wine vinegar
1 medium all-purpose potato, peeled and cut into bite sized pieces
1 teaspoon cumin

1. Wash the lentils. Place them in a large pot and cover with water. Add the Bay leaves, parsley, and bacon. Bring to a boil, reduce the heat, cover, and simmer 45 minutes.

2. Meanwhile, in a skillet over medium heat, heat the oil. Saute the onions, carrots, and garlic until the onion is wilted. Turn off the heat.

3. Stir in the paprika. Add this mixture to the lentils, then add the salt and pepper to taste, sausage, wine vinegar, potatoes and cumin. Cover and cook 45 minutes more, or until the lentils and potatoes are done.

Makes 6 servings

OLD FORT WILLIAM

During the early 1800's, Old Fort William was the inland headquarters for the vast fur trading empire of Canada's North West Company. Today it is a living museum just outside the city of Thunder Bay, Ontario. Historians have recreated 125 acres of trading post, with all the individual facilities that existed almost 200 years ago. Members of The Old Fort William staff, dressed in period costume, go about the same tasks that occupied the original residents of the Fort.

Of particular interest to me was the authentic reproduction of the pioneer cooking facilities. Visitors can clearly see how kitchen work was carried out for the hundreds of trappers, settlers, Native American Indians, military personnel and company employees that lived and worked at the original Fort William.

During my visit to the Fort, I was particularly impressed with their cafeteria facility, which is open to the public and reproduces old recipes. The food was simple, straightforward and tasted great. On the following pages are the period recipes for two of the dishes that were very popular during the time that the Fort was most active.

PEA SOUP
OLD FORT WILLIAM
THUNDER BAY, ONTARIO

1 pound green split peas
1/4 pound bacon, cut into bite sized pieces
1 medium onion, diced
2 carrots, peeled and diced
1 turnip, peeled and diced
1 medium potato, peeled and diced
1 teaspoon dry mustard
1 teaspoon Tabasco sauce
6 cups water
Salt and freshly ground black pepper

1. Pour hot water over the split peas and soak for one hour.

2. In a 6-quart saucepan, cook the bacon and onion over medium heat or until the onion is transparent. Add the carrots, turnip and potato.

3. Drain and rinse the split peas, add to the saucepan along with the mustard, Tabasco and water. Add salt and pepper to taste.

4. Cook one hour.

5. Remove one-half of the liquid and vegetables, and place in a blender or processor. Puree until smooth. Recombine the pureed portion with the unblended soup and serve.

Makes 6 servings

BEEF STEW
OLD FORT WILLIAM
THUNDER BAY, ONTARIO

3 tablespoons vegetable oil
1 large onion, diced
1 red or green bell pepper, seeds and ribs removed and coarsely chopped
$1/4$ pound fresh green beans
1 carrot, sliced into $1/2$-inch rounds
1 teaspoon minced garlic
1 pound lean beef, cut into bite sized cubes
2 potatoes, unpeeled, cut into bite sized pieces
1 cup uncooked brown rice
6 cups beef stock
$1/2$ teaspoon thyme
$1/2$ teaspoon rosemary
Salt and freshly ground black pepper

1. In a 6-quart saucepan, heat the oil over medium heat. Saute the onion, pepper, green beans, carrot and garlic for three minutes.

2. Add the beef and saute until lightly browned

3. Add potatoes, rice, beef stock and spices.

4. Bring to a boil, reduce heat and simmer for one hour. Season with salt and pepper to taste.

Makes 6 servings

PARISIAN ONION SOUP
RITZ HOTEL
PARIS, FRANCE

The Ritz Hotel is a monument commemorating the work of two men. One was Cesar Ritz, a famous hotel director and the other was Auguste Escoffier, a preeminent chef of the late 1800's. Together Ritz and Escoffier revolutionized the hotel and restaurant business. They introduced a level of luxury that had never before been available to the general public. So important were their contributions that Ritz's name became part of the international vocabulary for elegance. When we say something is ritzy, we are actually referring to the way Cesar Ritz would have done it. Today the traditions of both men live on in Paris's Ritz Hotel. A perfect example is the hotel's recipe for Parisian Onion Soup.

3 tablespoons butter
3 large onions, thinly sliced
1 teaspoon flour
Three 10 1/2-ounce cans condensed beef consomme
1 Bay leaf
Freshly grated black pepper
12 thin slices French bread
1 cup shredded Swiss or Gruyere cheese

1. Melt the butter in a 6-quart saucepan. Add the onions and cook over medium heat until they turn a deep golden color, 10 to 15 minutes. Meanwhile, preheat the broiler.

2. Stir the flour into the onions and let cook for 2 minutes.

3. Add the consomme, along with 3 cans of water. Use the consomme can as the measure. Add the Bay leaf. Bring to a boil. Lower the heat and let simmer for 10 minutes. Stir in the black pepper to taste. Remove the Bay leaf and discard.

4. Divide the soup into 6 heatproof bowls. Top each with 2 slices of bread and 2 to 3 tablespoons of cheese. Place the bowls under the broiler until cheese is bubbly and brown, 1 to 2 minutes.

Makes 6 servings

FISH CHOWDER
GRASS RIVER LODGE
REED LAKE, WINNIPEG, CANADA

Grass River Lodge is located 450 miles northwest of Winnipeg, Canada on scenic Reed Lake. The area is well known among fishermen for its large northerns, walleye and lake trout. Ike Enns owns and runs the lodge. He has been a fishing bush pilot for over 20 years and his wife Liz has been coming up with seafood recipes for just as long. The following chowder was cooked up during my visit to the Lodge in August of 1989. Bannock, a form of biscuit or doughnut that was popular in Scotland during the 19th century and brought to the New World by explorers, was served along with the chowder. A recipe for Buttermilk Bannock is on page 116.

3 tablespoons butter or margarine
1 medium onion, chopped
$^1/_4$ cup chopped celery
1 Bay leaf
1 teaspoon marjoram
3 cups milk
3 potatoes, peeled and diced
1 pound cod fillets (or any thick-fleshed white fish)

1. In a heavy saucepan over medium heat, melt the butter and saute the onion and the celery until the onion is tender but not browned, about 2 minutes.

2. Add the Bay leaf and the marjoram and saute for another 2 minutes.

3. Add the milk and the diced potatoes and cook over medium-low heat until the potatoes are tender but not mushy, about 15 minutes.

4. Meanwhile, cut the fish fillets into 2-inch pieces and when the potatoes are almost cooked, add the fish. Cook for about 3 minutes, until the fish is cooked through. Be careful not to stir the soup too vigorously or the fish will break-up into flakes. Remove and discard the Bay leaf and serve.

Makes 4 to 6 servings

PUERTO RICAN FISH STEW
LA MONSERRATE SEAPORT RESTAURANT
PONCE, PUERTO RICO

The southern coast of Puerto Rico faces the Caribbean sea and creates one of the islands most picturesque environments. Throughout the world, wherever the sea meets the sand, the seafood meets the sauce pot. In France it is called Bouillabaisse, in Italy it is called Cacciucco, in Puerto Rico it is called Asopao.

One of the masters of Puerto Rican coastal cooking is Margie Velazquez, who owns La Monserrate Seaport Restaurant just outside the city of Ponce. When I asked her how she learned to cook, she told me "from watching cooking on television." Right away I had to love her. But I was curious to see how the activity on the tube translated to the table. It's one thing to watch television and cook at home, it's quite another to cook in a restaurant. She proved her skill with the following recipe.

2 tablespoons butter
2 tablespoons vegetable oil
1 medium onion, chopped
1 small green bell pepper, chopped
2 cloves garlic, minced
$1/2$ pound firm, white-fleshed fish, cut in 1-inch chunks
12 ounces lobster meat, fresh or frozen and thawed
$1/2$ pound sea scallops
$1/2$ pound shrimp, peeled and cleaned
1 Bay leaf
16 ounces clam juice
$1/2$ cup uncooked rice
One 8-ounce can tomato sauce
$1/2$ teaspoon crushed red pepper flakes
Salt and freshly ground black pepper

1. Heat the butter and oil in a 6-quart saucepan, over medium heat. Add the onion, pepper and garlic. Cook until the onion is soft and translucent, about 7 minutes.

2. Add shellfish and fish. Cook, stirring occasionally, for about 5 minutes.

3. Add the Bay leaf and clam juice and bring to a boil. Lower the heat and let simmer for 10 minutes.

4. Stir in the rice. Cover and let simmer until rice is tender, about 20 minutes.

5. Add the tomato sauce and red pepper. Simmer 2 minutes. Season to taste with salt and pepper. Remove and discard the Bay leaf.

Makes 6 servings

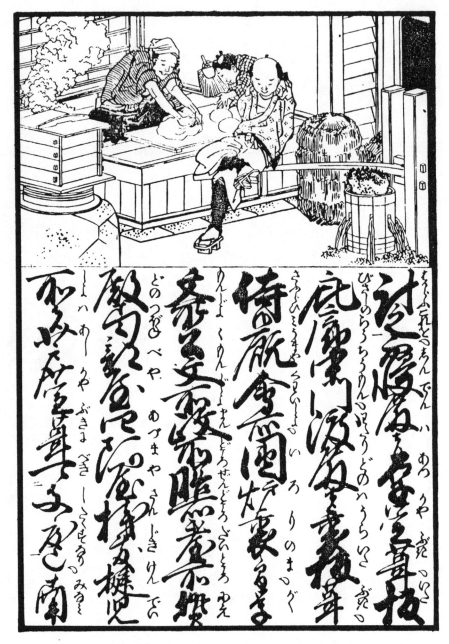

Hokusai Illustration for a Japanese Cookbook

FISH & SEAFOOD

KING OF HEARTS

Oscar was the King of Norway during the early 1900's. He was an okay king, and the people accepted him. But he was not a famous king. Not like B.B. King or Elvis. Then one day he put his picture on a sardine can and suddenly everyone knew King Oscar. And for good reason, too.

Sardines are one of the greatest natural sources of bone-building calcium. They provide potassium, magnesium, iron, zinc and iodine. They contain Vitamin B, Vitamin D and lots of protein. They are also packed with Omega 3. Omega 3 is a type of fish oil that appears to help reduce the risk of heart disease. Sardines could make old King Oscar the king of hearts.

The best sardines are made from a fish called a Brisling. They are netted at the point in the year when they are most flavorful and then lightly smoked over oak wood fires to enhance their delicate taste. I don't know if it's true, but I heard that King Oscar was working on a song about his favorite sardine recipe and the title was *Love Me Tender*.

BAKED SARDINES
AND MARINATED ARTICHOKES
OSLO, NORWAY

2 cans sardines (about 4 ounces each), drained
2 jars (about 6 ounces each) marinated artichokes
2 tablespoons olive oil
$1/2$ cup fresh bread crumbs
1 tablespoon chopped parsley
$1/2$ lemon, sliced

1. Preheat the oven to 350° F.

2. Arrange the sardines in the center of an 8-inch baking dish. Slightly drain the artichokes and arrange around the sardines.

3. Sprinkle with olive oil, bread crumbs then parsley. Arrange the lemon slices on top.

4. Bake for 15 to 20 minutes until hot.

Makes 4 servings

King Oscar

SARDINES WITH ZUCCHINI AND STUFFING
OSLO, NORWAY

2 cups fresh bread crumbs
$1/4$ cup grated Parmesan cheese
$1/4$ cup chopped parsley
$1/2$ cup heavy cream
1 egg, beaten
1 clove garlic, minced
$1/2$ teaspoon salt
$1/2$ teaspoon freshly ground black pepper
Dash ground nutmeg
$1/2$ pound zucchini, (about 2 medium zucchini), thinly sliced
2 cans sardines, (about 4 ounces each), drained

1. Preheat the oven to 350° F.

2. In a medium bowl combine all ingredients except the zucchini and sardines.

3. In an 8-inch ovenproof baking dish arrange the zucchini slices around the edge of the dish. Place the drained sardines in the center. Place the stuffing over the sardines, slightly overlapping onto the zucchini.

4. Bake for 20 minutes until the stuffing is lightly browned.

Makes 6 servings

BROILED SALMON WITH AVOCADO SAUCE
FEDJE FISH FARM
NORWAY

The coastal waters of the north Atlantic are home to the salmon farmers of Norway. These hardy individuals have mastered the very complex techniques of constructing giant floating platforms that contain nets in which the salmon are raised. The system is made possible by the warm water current that comes up to Norway from the Gulf of Mexico. This recipe combines elements from the gastronomic culture of each country involved ... an avocado and salsa sauce from Mexico topped with a fillet of Norwegian salmon.

2 ripe avocados
The juice of 2 lemons
2 tablespoons sour cream (or low-fat yogurt)
$^1/_2$ bunch watercress
$^1/_2$ cup prepared salsa
Salt and freshly ground black pepper
1 pound salmon fillets
Olive oil for brushing
Lemon wedges for serving

1. In a medium bowl, mash the avocado meat until you have a "chunky" mixture. Add the lemon juice and sour cream and mix well to combine.

2. In a processor, puree the watercress and add to the avocado mixture. Fold in the salsa and season to taste. Chill the mixture until needed.

3. Preheat the broiler. Brush the salmon fillet with olive oil and broil under high heat approximately 4 minutes on each side, depending on the thickness of the fish.

4. Serve the fish with the avocado sauce on the side and wedges of lemon. It goes well with rice or boiled new potatoes and a green vegetable like broccoli or green beans.

Makes 4 servings

SAUTEED SALMON WITH REMOULADE SAUCE
FEDJE FISH FARM
NORWAY

2 tablespoons vegetable oil
1 pound salmon fillets
Salt and freshly ground pepper
Lemon wedges for serving

1. In a large non-stick skillet, place the oil and heat.

2. Season the salmon to taste and saute for about 3 minutes on each side, depending on the thickness of the fillets.

3. Serve with Remoulade Sauce on the side and lemon wedges.

Makes 4 servings

REMOULADE SAUCE

6 tablespoons prepared Creole mustard or other hot and spicy mustard
1 teaspoon prepared white horseradish
3 tablespoons chopped garlic
$^1/_3$ cup chopped celery
$^1/_3$ cup chopped dill pickles
3 tablespoons chopped fresh parsley
$^1/_3$ cup chopped scallions
$^2/_3$ cup vegetable oil
$^1/_3$ cup white wine vinegar
Dash of Worcestershire sauce
5 drops of Tabasco sauce

1. In a mixing bowl combine the mustard, horseradish, garlic, celery, pickles, parsley and scallions. Blend together. Whisk in the remaining ingredients.

Makes 1 $^1/_2$ cups

CODFISH CAKES
AMADEUS RESTAURANT
OLD SAN JUAN, PUERTO RICO

The island of Puerto Rico has been inhabited for well over 2,000 years. The first residents were the Taino Indians, then the Spanish, the West Africans, and finally, the Americans. Each of these groups brought with them their traditional approach to food.

Today, the island serves up a mixture produced from these influences. You can see this at the Amadeus Restaurant in the old city of San Juan. Run by the brothers Ramirez, the restaurant menu clearly illustrates the influences of each period in the island's history. The Taino were great fishermen, and are represented by the Tuna Kebabs (page 21); the Spanish brought Codfish Cakes (below), the West Africans contributed thick soups (page 6) and the Americans, pizza (page 120).

3/4 **pound codfish, cooked and flaked**
1/4 **cup chopped onion, sauteed and cooled**
1 1/2 **cups all-purpose flour**
Salt and freshly ground black pepper
3 **cloves garlic, finely chopped**
1/2 **tablespoon dried oregano**
1 **teaspoon baking powder**
1 1/2 **cups water**
Salsa for serving

1. In a small bowl, combine the cooked fish and the sauteed onions. Set aside.

2. In a large bowl, combine the flour, salt and pepper to taste, garlic, oregano and baking powder. Add the water and mix well. Add the codfish mixture, stir gently and let sit (at room temperature) for approximately 30 minutes.

3. Onto a non-stick skillet, using a 1/8-cup measure, drop the batter to form little cakes and saute for 2 to 3 minutes on each side until the pancakes are golden brown. Serve immediately with the salsa of your choice.

Makes approximately 20 cakes

TUNA KEBABS
AMADEUS RESTAURANT
OLD SAN JUAN, PUERTO RICO

This recipe shows the cultural influence of the Taino Indians, who were the first inhabitants of Puerto Rico and well known as great fishermen. These kebabs are perfect for an outdoor barbecue.

¹/₈ cup sesame oil
¹/₄ cup olive oil
¹/₂ tablespoon dry tarragon
1 teaspoon fresh lemon juice
Salt and freshly ground black pepper
1 pound fresh tuna, cut into 1-inch pieces
1 green bell pepper, ribs and seeds removed, cut into 8 pieces
8 cherry tomatoes
4 tablespoons toasted sesame seeds (optional)

1. In a medium bowl combine the oils, tarragon, lemon juice and salt and pepper to taste. Add the tuna to the oil mixture. Marinate at least 3 hours in the refrigerator.

2. Pre-heat the broiler. On four kabob skewers, thread the tuna alternately with the pepper and tomatoes.

3. Broil (or grill) under high heat 5 to 6 minutes or until the tuna is browned outside and still slightly rare inside.

4. Remove the kabobs from the broiler and sprinkle with toasted sesame seeds if used. Serve immediately.

NOTE: Toasting the sesame seeds brings out their rich nutty flavor. To toast the seeds, sprinkle them in a dry skillet (preferable a non-stick one) and place over moderate heat. Stir constantly until the seeds are golden brown, about 2 to 3 minutes.

Makes 4 servings

GRATIN OF WALLEYE ON SPINACH
BANBURY HOUSE
WOLSELEY, SASKATCHEWAN, CANADA

Saskatchewan, one of the provinces of Canada, is a fisherman's paradise. The lakes, rivers and streams of this unspoiled northern region are home to trout, northern pike, whitefish, grayling and walleye. The walleye is a tender white-fleshed fish that is perfect for pan frying. The following recipe comes from Ernest Boehm, the chef and owner of Banbury House Inn. Served with rice, it makes a substantial meal.

1 pound walleye fillets (or flounder) fresh or frozen
Salt and pepper for seasoning
2 tablespoons vegetable oil
The juice of 1 lemon
2 tablespoons butter or margarine
1 small onion, chopped
One 10-ounce package frozen spinach, thawed, chopped and
    drained
Salt and freshly ground pepper
1/4 teaspoon nutmeg
2 small tomatoes, thinly sliced
1/2 cup shredded Gruyere cheese (or mozzarella)
Cooked rice for serving

1. Preheat oven to 375° F. Salt and pepper the fillets. In a large skillet heat the oil and when it is hot add the fillets. Pour the lemon juice over the fish. Cook for approximately 2 minutes, then turn the fish over and cook for about 2 minutes more. Remove the fillets to a plate.

2. In the same pan that the fish was cooked in, melt the butter and add the onion and spinach. Season to taste and add the nutmeg. Saute for 2 minutes and remove from the heat.

3. In a heatproof baking dish or casserole, spread out the spinach mixture and top with the fillets. Place the tomatoes on top of the fillets and sprinkle the cheese over the fish. Place the dish in the oven and bake for about 6 minutes or until the cheese is melted and the fish is heated through. Serve immediately.

Makes 4 servings

A Royal Picnic

PHARAOH'S FISH
HARRODS FOOD HALLS
LONDON, ENGLAND

In 1985 Mohamed Al Fayed, an Egyptian businessman, purchased control of Harrods Department Store in London, England. Since then, Mohamed has spent many millions of dollars improving and restoring this British landmark. One of the most important areas in Harrods consist of the giant Food Halls which offer the finest food products from all over the world. A while ago, Mohamed and I were talking about the tastes of our childhood, recipes that we remember from our youth with great affection. One of Mohamed's favorites was a dish from Alexandria, Egypt, called Pharaoh's Fish. He demonstrated the recipe right on the selling floor of Harrods.

2 whole, cleaned red snapper about 2 pounds each (or other whole firm white fleshed fish)
4 springs fresh parsley
4 sprigs fresh oregano (4 teaspoons dried)
1 small onion, chopped
4 tablespoons vegetable oil
3 cups bran
Lemon wedges for serving

1. Heat the oven to 375° F. Place a rack in the bottom of a baking dish.

2. In the cavity of each fish place 2 parsley sprigs, the oregano and the chopped onion. Lightly brush each side of the fish with the oil.

3. In a large flat dish (or on a cookie sheet) place the bran for coating the fish. Place the fish on the bran and press well to make sure the bran adheres to the fish. Turn the fish over and coat the second side. Repeat with the other fish.

4. Place the fish on the rack in the baking dish and bake uncovered for approximately 35 minutes or until the fish is cooked to the desired degree of doneness.

5. Serve immediately with lemon wedges.

Makes 4 servings

NOTE: In earlier times, it was common to coat a fish with mud from a river bank in order to hold in the food's moisture during cooking. The mud would harden during the cooking time and be cracked off just prior to serving. In the above recipe, oat bran is used to do the same job. If you would like to be *really* authentic in your recipe for Pharaoh's Fish, after completing the recipe above follow the instructions below.

Make a mixture of 3 cups of water, 2 cups of white vinegar and ¼ cup of chopped garlic. When the fish has finished cooking, place each whole fish in this mixture for approximately 2 minutes. The skin will peel off easily.

CODFISH SALAD
CONDADO PLAZA HOTEL & CASINO
SAN JUAN, PUERTO RICO

A Le Lo Lai Festival is a celebration of Puerto Rican food, music and dance and almost every evening you'll find one taking place in the hotels of San Juan. The foods presented are the traditional dishes of the island, including the following Codfish Salad, Paella, page 82 and Piña Colada, page 125.

1 **pound cooked codfish, chilled and flaked**
2 **large tomatoes, chopped**
2 **green bell peppers, chopped**
$^{1}/_{3}$ **cup chopped fresh cilantro (or parsley)**
$^{1}/_{2}$ **teaspoon cayenne pepper**
$^{1}/_{4}$ **teaspoon salt**

1. In a large bowl, gently combine all of the above ingredients, being careful not to mash the fish. Chill well before serving with Cumin Vinaigrette or Light Lemon Mayonnaise.

Makes 4 servings

CUMIN VINAIGRETTE

1/4 cup sherry vinegar
1 teaspoon prepared mustard
1 tablespoon chopped shallots
1 teaspoon ground cumin
$1/4$ teaspoon salt
$1/4$ teaspoon freshly ground black pepper
$1/4$ cup olive oil
$1/2$ cup vegetable oil

1. In a blender or food processor, combine the vinegar, mustard, shallots, cumin, salt and pepper. With the motor running, drizzle in the oils and process until smooth. Chill before tossing with the salad.

Makes 4 servings

LIGHT LEMON MAYONNAISE

Juice of 2 lemons
1 cup reduced calorie mayonnaise
$1/2$ teaspoon cumin
Salt and freshly ground black pepper to taste

1. In a small bowl, combine all ingredients. Chill well before tossing gently.

Makes 4 servings

MINAKI SHORE LUNCH

The Minaki Lodge is one of the world's great wilderness resorts. Their specialty is taking guests off into the local lakes either by boat or float plane for a day of fishing. About noon time, your guide sets up a fire on the lake side and prepares a shore lunch. The guides' lunch box gives a new meaning to the word optimism. There are beans, onions, potatoes, batter and bread, but if you don't catch a fish there's no main dish. The guides, however, assured me that that had never happened, and I was no exception. The preparation is as follows: A cup of oil is heated in a large saute pan. New potatoes, cut into bit sized pieces go into the oil. After a few minutes of cooking, sliced onions are added. Ten minutes later the potatoes and onions are strained out of the cooking oil. A small bucket is used to make a dipping batter for the fish. The fish fillets are coated with the batter and fried in a second pan of heated oil. When the fish is cooked through, about ten minutes, the fillets are drained on paper toweling. A can of baked beans is heated in the coals. Lunch consists of fish, potatoes and onions, baked beans, bread and fresh air.

BEER BATTER FOR FISH

$^1/_2$ **cup flour**
Pinch of salt
1 tablespoon melted butter
1 egg, beaten
$^1/_2$ **cup beer**

1. Mix the flour and salt into a mixing bowl. Stir in the butter and egg. Add the beer gradually, stirring only until the mixture is smooth.

OREGON COAST TUNA WITH MUSTARD SAUCE
SALISHAN LODGE
GLENEDEN, OREGON

6 tablespoons minced shallots (or onion)
2 tablespoons vegetable oil plus some for brushing
6 tablespoons chopped fresh thyme (3 tablespoons dried)
Salt and freshly ground black pepper
2 cups white wine
6 tablespoons prepared mustard (preferably Dijon style)
4 tuna steaks about 1 inch thick (about 4 ounces each)

1. Make the sauce: In a skillet over medium-high heat, saute the shallots in 2 tablespoons of oil for approximately 2 minutes. Add the thyme, salt and black pepper to taste and continue cooking until the shallots are cooked and the skillet is almost dry.

2. Add the wine and stir, scraping up any browned bits from the bottom of the pan. Cook for approximately 4 minutes to slightly reduce the wine.

3. Gently whisk in the mustard and cook for another 2 minutes, reducing the heat to medium-low. Keep warm.

4. Pre-heat the broiler. Lightly brush the tuna steaks with oil and broil (or grill) for about 3 minutes on each side until the desired degree of doneness is reached.

5. Place a generous serving of the sauce on each dinner plate and top with the tuna.

Makes 4 servings

SALISHAN LODGE

NEWPORT, OREGON SHRIMP

For over 100 years, Newport, Oregon, has been one of the most important fishing harbors on the West Coast. The boats bring in salmon, sole, red snapper and shrimp. Shrimp is a ten-legged crustacean and the most popular shellfish in the United States. We eat over 500 million pounds of shrimp each year, and that is more than any other country in the world. We have eaten shrimp in this country as far back as we have recorded information. Native American Indians, colonists, pioneers ... wherever there was access to an ocean ... shrimp popped onto the local menu. Local is the key word, because fresh shrimp do not last very long, as a result, for centuries, shrimp was truly a local specialty. In 1917, we began putting refrigerators on the fishing boats and in the 1950's we began freezing shrimp for shipment. Today Newport shrimp are shipped all over the world. Local cooks use them to make some fabulous shrimp dishes, the following two recipes are typical examples.

The recipe on the next page comes from the kitchens of the shrimpers in the harbor of Newport, Oregon. The ingredient list is a short guide to many of the cultures that have influenced the cooking of our Pacific states: shrimp from the Native Americans, wine from the Spanish missionaries, pea pods from the Chinese immigrants, chili from Mexico, and cooking in a bag from the French (who came for the gold rush).

PAUPIETTES OF SOLE WITH SHRIMP
NEWPORT, OREGON

Four 4-ounce fillets of sole (or other thin white fish)
8 medium shrimp, cleaned and deveined
8 pea pods, cleaned and steamed
1/4 cup white wine
1/2 cup water plus 2 tablespoons
The zest and juice of 2 lemons
2 tablespoons rice wine vinegar
1 tablespoon chili sauce
1 teaspoon sesame oil
1 tablespoon cornstarch
1 tablespoon vegetable oil
2 tablespoons freshly grated ginger
2 cloves garlic, minced

1. Preheat the oven to 325° F. Gently pat the fillets dry and lay them out lengthwise with the dark side of the fish facing upwards. Place 2 shrimp and 2 pea pods in the center of each fillet so that the ends of each stick out slightly. Roll up the fillets and place them in a baking dish.

2. Pour the wine and 1/2 cup of water into the dish and place the fish in the oven. Cook for approximately 12 minutes until the fish is cooked.

3. Meanwhile, make the sauce: Into a small bowl grate the lemon zest and then add the juice. Add the vinegar, chili sauce, sesame oil, cornstarch and remaining water.

4. In a small saucepan heat the vegetable oil and saute the ginger and garlic for about 1 minute. Add the sauce mixture into the saucepan and continue stirring until thickened.

5. When the fish is done, remove it from the oven and pour about 3/4 cup of the poaching liquid into the saucepan. Reheat the sauce gently, remove the fish to a serving dish and spoon the sauce over it.

Makes 4 servings

STIR-FRIED SHRIMP WITH CASHEWS AND CHINESE VEGETABLES NEWPORT, OREGON

During the mid 1800's, thousands of Chinese workers immigrated to the Western part of the United States to help construct the railroads. Their gastronomic influence can be seen in many West Coast recipes, including the following one from Newport, Oregon. This dish and some brown rice, and you have an excellent meal which is low in fat and high in valuable complex carbohydrates.

3 tablespoons water
1 tablespoon cornstarch
1 tablespoon soy sauce (low-sodium if possible)
1 teaspoon sugar
2 tablespoons vegetable oil
1 small head Chinese cabbage, washed and roughly chopped
1 bunch scallions, washed and sliced on the diagonal into 1/4-inch pieces
1 pound medium shrimp, shelled and deveined
1/4 teaspoon ground ginger
1/2 teaspoon red pepper flakes
One 15-ounce can straw mushrooms (optional)
Cashews for serving
Cooked brown rice for serving

1. In a small bowl combine the water, cornstarch, soy sauce and the sugar. Set aside.

2. In a large skillet or wok, heat the oil and stir fry the cabbage and scallions for 2 minutes. Add 1 tablespoon of the cornstarch mixture and continue cooking for 1 minute. Remove from the skillet to a serving platter and keep warm.

3. In the same skillet (add a little more oil if necessary), fry the shrimp, ginger and red pepper for 2 minutes. Add the mushrooms and the remaining cornstarch mixture. Cook for another two minutes and spoon over the vegetables on the serving dish. Top with the cashews and serve.

Makes 4 servings

GRILLED HADDOCK
WITH SAUTEED VEGETABLES
HOTEL NORGE ♦ BERGEN, NORWAY

3 tablespoons olive oil
1 small onion, chopped
1 small red bell pepper, chopped
1 small fennel bulb, chopped (or 1/2 cup chopped celery)
1/2 small eggplant, peeled and chopped (about 1 cup)
1 small zucchini, chopped
3 garlic cloves, minced
One 10-ounce package frozen spinach, thawed, chopped and
   drained
1/8 cup white wine
Salt and pepper to taste
4 whole carrots, steamed
1 pound haddock fillets (or other firm fleshed white fish)

1. In a large skillet, heat the oil and add the onion. Cook 3 minutes and then add the bell pepper, fennel and eggplant. Cook 4 minutes stirring constantly to keep the vegetables from sticking to the bottom of the pan. Add the zucchini, garlic and spinach and continue cooking for 3 minutes. Add the white wine, cook for 3 more minutes and season to taste. Place the cooked carrots on top of the vegetables and keep warm while you cook the fish.

2. Grill the haddock over high heat or place under a pre-heated broiler for 4 to 5 minutes on each side, depending on the thickness of the fish.

3. Place the vegetables on a serving dish, top with the fillets and garnish with the whole carrots.

NOTE: This is a very pretty dish for home entertaining and is very easy to prepare since the vegetable mixture can be made early in the day and then reheated before serving. Simply bring the vegetables to room temperature before warming.

Makes 4 servings

SHRIMP "BUNNIES" WITH CREOLE SAUCE

Jacques Pepin was born in France and began his cooking career at the age of 13 when he apprenticed at his parents' restaurant in the city of Lyon. During the 1950's, he was the personal chef to three Presidents of France. Today, he lives in Madison, Connecticut, where he writes books and teaches the techniques of good cooking. The following recipe, which makes quite an amazing presentation, is adapted from his book The Art of Cooking, Volume I, *published by Knopf.*

Shrimp:
24 shrimp (about 1 1/2 pounds of 16 - 18 count shrimp; i.e. there are 16 - 18 shrimp to the pound)
1/2 cup dry white wine
1/4 teaspoon salt

Sauce:
1 tablespoon butter
1 cup coarsely chopped onions
1 cup coarsely chopped celery
1 teaspoon chopped jalapeño pepper
2 cups chopped tomatoes
1 cup water
1/2 teaspoon salt

Garlic Spinach:
2 tablespoons olive oil
3 cloves garlic, chopped (1 tablespoon)
1 pound spinach, stems removed, washed
1/2 teaspoon salt
1/4 teaspoon freshly ground black pepper

1. Shell the shrimp, leaving only the shell around the tail attached. Reserve the shells you have removed.

2. Curl each shrimp around to form the "body" of the "bunny." Cut a thin slice from the base so the "bunny" can "sit" firmly in the cooking skillet and on the plate.

3. Curl the shrimp into a tight bunny shape. Secure with a toothpick, pushing it from the "tail" through the "head."

4. To make the sauce: Heat the butter in a saucepan. When hot, add the reserved shells and saute for 2 to 3 minutes. Add the onions, celery, and jalapeño pepper, and cook a few minutes. Add the tomatoes, water, and salt, bring to a boil, and cook for 10 minutes. Push the sauce through a food mill fitted with the small screen.

5. Stand the "bunnies" up side by side in a small buttered saucepan. They should fit fairly tightly so they don't fall over. Pour the wine around the "bunnies" and sprinkle with 1/4 teaspoon salt. Bring to a boil, cover, and let boil for 10 to 15 seconds. Leave the cover on and remove the pan to the side of the stove. Using the lid to hold the "bunnies" in the pan, pour off the cooking juices and add them to the sauce. Cook the sauce and liquid together for 8 to 10 minutes to reduce. Keep the shrimp covered in a warm place while preparing the spinach.

6. In a large saucepan, heat the olive oil. When hot, add the garlic and saute for about 1 minute. Add the spinach, still wet from washing, and the salt and pepper. Cover and cook about 1 minute. Uncover and continue cooking for 1 to 2 minutes to get rid of most of the liquid. With a slotted spoon, lift out the spinach and arrange portions of it in the center of the individual plates. Surround with the red sauce, place 4 "bunnies" on top of the spinach "nest," pressing down to make them stand upright. Serve immediately.

Makes 6 servings

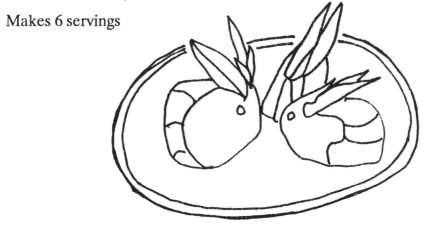

OYSTERS AL FAYED
RITZ HOTEL
PARIS, FRANCE

Mohamed Al Fayed was born in Alexandria, Egypt. For many years he worked in his family businesses, which included shipping, hotels, property and finance. The hotel experiences made a considerable impression on Mohamed and today he owns the Ritz Hotel in Paris. The Ritz is one of the world's most magnificent hotels and Mohamed continues to improve its facilities. Recently, we were talking about recipes that each of us have created to meet our personal tastes. Mine, of course, was based on ice cream and chocolate; Mohamed's work has a foundation of oysters and caviar. Oysters Al Fayed makes a very impressive and interesting start to any meal.

Herb Garlic Butter:
5 tablespoons plus 1 teaspoon sweet butter, softened
1 tablespoon fresh parsley, minced
2 garlic cloves, minced

The juice of 2 limes
4 tablespoons brandy
16 fresh oysters, preferably Belon
8 ounces cooked lobster or crabmeat
2 medium tomatoes, peeled, seeded and diced
5 tablespoons plus 1 teaspoon catsup
5 tablespoons plus 1 teaspoon caviar
6 tablespoons grated Parmesan cheese

1. To make the herb butter: In a small bowl, combine all the ingredients and mix together to a smooth paste. Set aside

2. In a medium bowl, combine the lime juice and the brandy.

3. Shuck the oysters and place the oyster meat in the lime/brandy mixture. Discard the top shell and rinse the bottom shell of all sand and debris.

4. In each shell, layer the following ingredients in the following order: 1 teaspoon of herb butter, 1 drained oyster, 1/2 ounce cooked lobster meat, a bit of diced tomato, 1 teaspoon catsup and 1 teaspoon caviar. Flatten the mound slightly with the back of a spoon and sprinkle 1/2 tablespoon of Parmesan cheese over the top.

5. Place the oysters on a broiler pan. Place the pan into a heated broiler for 3 to 4 minutes until the cheese is lightly browned.

Makes 4 servings

Oyster Eaters.

OVEN POACHED HALIBUT WITH BROCCOLI AND RED PEPPER SAUCE
RITZ HOTEL HEALTH CLUB
PARIS, FRANCE

Red Pepper Sauce:
4 red bell peppers
Juice of 1 lemon
1/8 cup olive oil
1/4 cup sour cream (or low-fat yogurt)
Salt and freshly ground black pepper

Halibut:
1 pound halibut fillets, fresh or frozen (or other firm white fish)
1/8 cup white wine
1/4 cup water
1 bunch broccoli, cooked, and cut into small pieces

To Make the Sauce:

1. Place the peppers over a flame on a gas burner or under the broiler. Turn them until most of the skin is blackened and blistered. Place the peppers in a plastic bag and seal the opening. Keep the peppers in the closed bag for 5 minutes. Remove the peppers from the bag and rub off the skins under cold water.

2. Cut the peppers open and remove the seeds and ribs.

3. Place the peppers in a food processor or blender and puree. Add the lemon juice, olive oil, and sour cream. Process until smooth, season with salt and pepper to taste and place in a saucepan until ready to use. (This can be done the day ahead and kept refrigerated until needed.)

To Make the Halibut:

1. Preheat the oven to 350° F.

2. Place the fillets in a shallow baking dish or casserole. Pour the wine and water over them. Cover the baking dish with foil and place in the oven for approximately 8 to 10 minutes or until the fish is cooked through.

3. Meanwhile, heat the sauce gently over low to moderate heat.

4. Place a serving of the sauce on each of 4 dinner plates. Put a serving of the broccoli in the center of the plate. Cover the broccoli with a halibut fillet and serve, passing the remaining sauce separately.

Makes 4 servings

STEAMED FISH FINGERS
RITZ HOTEL HEALTH CLUB
PARIS, FRANCE

The ancient Romans built spas all over Europe. And just to show us that the more things change, the more they are the same, the most modern and luxurious health club you could imagine was recently built in Roman style beneath the Ritz Hotel in Paris. There is a pool that would please a Roman Emperor. Massage and skin care areas that are fit for an empress. Exercise rooms that could build the body of a gladiator ... and a special menu that could teach nutrition to Nero. One of the most popular dishes at the Ritz Health Club is Steamed Fish Fingers. For other Ritz Health Club recipes see pages 38, 41 and 56.

4 ounces monkfish
4 ounces salmon
4 ounces swordfish
4 ounces fresh tuna
¹/₈ cup chopped fresh parsley (or 1 tablespoons dried)
¹/₈ cup soy sauce
¹/₄ cup water
1 tablespoon grated fresh ginger
1 tablespoon rice wine vinegar
The zest and juice of 1 orange

1. Cut each fish into 4 "fingers" and place in a steamer insert above 2 inches of water in the bottom of a pan with a tight fitting lid. Steam for about 4 minutes.

2. Meanwhile make the sauce: In a small saucepan, combine the parsley, soy sauce, water, ginger, vinegar, orange zest and juice. Heat gently.

3. Place the fish in a tent shape in the center of a dish and pour the sauce on top. Serve immediately. This dish is especially nice when served on a bed of steamed kale or on a nest of spinach pasta.

Makes 4 servings

SAUTEED SHRIMP WITH VEGETABLE SALAD
RITZ HOTEL HEALTH CLUB ♦ PARIS, FRANCE

<u>Vinaigrette:</u>
$^1/_8$ cup fresh lime juice
2 cloves garlic, minced
$^1/_8$ cup water
$^1/_4$ cup olive oil
$^1/_8$ cup chopped fresh cilantro (or parsley)
Salt and freshly ground black pepper

16 jumbo shrimp (or 4 lobster tails sliced lengthwise into 4
   slices)
$^1/_4$ teaspoon cayenne pepper
$^1/_2$ teaspoon cumin
$^1/_4$ teaspoon salt
$^1/_4$ teaspoon black pepper
2 cups cooked green beans
2 medium red onions, sliced thin
Vegetable oil or non-stick cooking spray

1. Make the vinaigrette: In a blender or processor, combine the juice, garlic and water. With the machine running, add the olive oil until well blended. Pour into a small saucepan and stir in the chopped cilantro. Season with salt and pepper to taste. Set aside.

2. In a small bowl, toss the shrimp with the spices and the salt and pepper and set aside.

3. Steam the vegetables for approximately 4 minutes.

4. Lightly coat a large non-stick skillet with vegetable oil (or use non-stick cooking spray) and heat well. Add the shrimp and saute until done, about 5 minutes. Be careful not to overcook or the shrimp will become tough.

5. In the center of a serving dish, place the french beans and the onions. Surround with the shrimp. Keep warm.

6. Bring the vinaigrette to a boil and pour over the salad. Serve immediately.

Makes 4 servings

Illustration from an English Cookbook printed for King John in 1711

POULTRY

CHICKEN AMARETTO
CHEZ MOUSTACHE ♦ AURORA, OREGON

Chez Moustache, a restaurant in Aurora, Oregon, does not have a pre-printed menu, which could mean a number of things. It could mean that the chef thinks you should eat what ever he's cooked and he doesn't want to discuss it, or the local printer could be on vacation, or the menu is so beautiful that they have all been taken by last night's customers. It could also mean that the chef likes to cook what he thinks would be just right for the night. Which, fortunately, is the actual case. The following recipe was prepared by chef Joel Miller.

4 tablespoons butter or margarine
2 chicken breasts, boned, skinned and split in half
³/₄ cup ground almonds, or your favorite nuts
¹/₄ cup Amaretto liqueur

1. Melt the butter in a skillet. Place the chicken breasts in the melted butter and saute over medium heat for 2 minutes. Cover the chicken breasts with the ground almonds, gently pressing them into the meat. Cook 2 more minutes.

2. Turn the chicken breasts on their other side and reduce the heat to low. Cook for approximately 3 minutes or to the desired degree of doneness.

3. Turn the heat up to moderately high and pour the Amaretto around the chicken breasts. Using a long match, very carefully ignite the liqueur and allow the alcohol to burn off. Gently swirl the pan until the flames subside and serve the chicken with some of the sauce.

Makes 4 servings

CHICKEN JAJOME
JAJOME TERRACE ♦ CAYEY, PUERTO RICO

A few years ago, the Puerto Rican government set up a program designed to protect and promote the gastronomic heritage of the island, it is called Mesones Gastronomicos, *which I like to translate as "the houses with the good food." The project consists of two dozen or so small restaurants, spread out over the island that specialize in the native foods of the region. A perfect example of* Mesones Gastronomicos *is Jajome Terrace in the central mountain range of the island. The restaurant sits at an altitude of 2,500 feet and the quality of its cooking is as elevated as its location. When I was there in July of 1989, the chef prepared Chicken Jajome.*

One 3-pound frying chicken, cut into 8 pieces, skin removed
2 cups orange juice
$^1/_2$ cup slivered almonds
$^3/_4$ cup raisins
3 tablespoons chutney (or apricot preserves)
1 teaspoon fresh thyme ($^1/_2$ teaspoon dried)
1 teaspoon curry powder
1 teaspoon cinnamon
Salt and freshly ground black pepper to taste
Cooked rice for serving

1. Preheat the oven to 375° F.

2. Place the chicken in a baking pan. Bake for 15 minutes to lightly brown.

3. Meanwhile, in a saucepan, combine all of the remaining ingredients and bring the mixture to a boil.

4. Remove the chicken from the oven and pour the liquid over the chicken. Cover the pan with aluminum foil and return the chicken to the oven for 30 minutes, until done.

Makes 4 servings

IDAHO POTATO & CURRIED CHICKEN SALAD
BOISE, IDAHO

Barbara Walters is the wife of Warren Walters, one of Idaho's most important potato growers. Recently, I stopped by their farm to talk about the history of potato growing in Idaho and to cook up this recipe. Quite simply, it is a marriage of a great potato salad and a great chicken salad.

4 Idaho potatoes, baked and cooled
3 cups cooked chicken, cut into bite-sized cubes
One 10-ounce package frozen peas, thawed
1 cup chopped celery
1 cup raisins
1/3 cup chopped scallions (green onion)
1 1/2 cups reduced calorie mayonnaise
1 to 2 tablespoons curry, depending on taste
Salt and freshly ground black pepper

1. Cut the cooked potatoes into bite-sized pieces but do not peel. Place into a large mixing bowl.

2. Add the chicken, thawed peas, celery, raisins and scallions. Set aside.

3. In a small mixing bowl combine the mayonnaise and the curry powder and season to taste. Mix until very well combined.

4. Pour the mayonnaise mixture over the potato salad and toss to coat the salad evenly. The salad can be served at room temperature or chilled in the refrigerator.

Makes 6 servings

NOTE: This is one of those potato salads that really improve with age. Make it a day ahead.

SUNDAY CHICKEN DINNER

Tired of vacationing in the urban sophistication of Europe? Bored with the beaches of the Caribbean? Do you find the mountains of the Alps monotonous? Time for something completely different? The Canadian province of Saskatchewan introduces you to the County Vacation Farm. Cavort with the cows. Dance till dawn with the ducks. Wallow in the wheat to your hearts content. Gamble with the geese. This is an unusual vacation, complete with an endless supply of fresh air. You will pass your time on real working farms where you can help with the chores, feed the chickens, milk the cows or pick the berries. They are places free of pollution and perfect for kids. They are also places to get a first-hand taste of what hardy farm cooking is all about. Pan-fried chicken served with gravy. Freshly whipped potatoes. Bowls of vegetables. Home-made jams. Breads and buns right out of the oven. All prepared by the friendly, down-to-earth folks who open their homes as vacation farms. Chicken, mashed potatoes and peas and carrots are my favorite Sunday meal, and when they're cooked right, they are unbeatable. The recipes on pages 47, 48 and 49 will give you all the fixings.

OVEN FRIED CHICKEN
COUNTRY VACATION FARMS
SASKATCHEWAN, CANADA

$1/2$ cup melted butter or margarine
1 frying chicken, about 3 pounds, skin removed, cut into 8 pieces
1 cup dry bread crumbs
1 teaspoon salt
$1/2$ teaspoon freshly ground black pepper
3 cloves of garlic, minced
1 teaspoon marjoram

1. Preheat oven to 375° F.

2. In a large bowl, drizzle the melted butter over the chicken pieces and toss well to coat them. Set aside.

3. On a large plate or board, mix the remaining ingredients.

4. Roll each piece of chicken in the breadcrumb mixture and place in a baking pan. Bake for approximately 45 minutes until the chicken is cooked through.

5. Remove the chicken to a serving dish and reserve the pan to make the gravy. Cover chicken with foil and keep warm while making the cream gravy.

Makes 4 servings

OLD FASHIONED CREAM GRAVY

1 cup chicken stock
$2/3$ cup heavy cream
2 teaspoons cornstarch mixed with 1 tablespoon warm water

1. Place the pan that the chicken was cooked in on top of the stove over moderate heat. Add the stock and stir, scraping up any browned bits.

2. Add the cream and continue to stir. Add the cornstarch mixture and stir until slightly thickened. Season to taste and serve with the chicken.

Makes 4 servings

OLD-FASHIONED MASHED POTATOES
COUNTRY VACATION FARMS
SASKATCHEWAN, CANADA

4 large baking potatoes
1 cup milk
4 tablespoons butter or margarine
Salt and freshly ground black pepper

1. Peel the potatoes, cut them into quarters, place them in a large pot and cover them with cold water. Cook until fork tender, about 30 minutes.

2. Remove the pot from the heat and drain the potatoes well.

3. In a large bowl, mash together the potatoes, milk and butter. Mash well. Season to taste. Serve immediately.

Makes 4 servings

NOTE: In today's convenience oriented kitchens, we may be tempted to "mash" our potatoes in a food processor. Resist this temptation. Potatoes contain gluten—much the same as flour does—by whipping them electronically, the gluten is developed into a gummy paste.

MINTED PEAS & CARROTS
COUNTRY VACATION FARMS
SASKATCHEWAN, CANADA

One 10-ounce package frozen peas
One 12-ounce bag baby carrots
1 tablespoon butter or margarine
4 tablespoons fresh mint (2 tablespoons dried), chopped

1. Thaw the peas and set aside.

2. Peel and clean the carrots. Steam the carrots until they are crisp-tender, about 5 minutes. Drain the carrots and run them under cold water to stop the cooking.

3. Just before serving, in a large skillet, melt the butter over moderate heat. Add the carrots and peas, tossing gently until heated through, about 3 minutes. Remove from the heat, toss with the mint and serve.

Makes 4 servings

CHICKEN WITH RICE
MIGUEL DOMENECH
SAN JUAN, PUERTO RICO

When tourists come to Puerto Rico, they see the elegant hotels, the beautiful beaches, the 16th and 17th century architecture of Old San Juan, the Fortress El Moro, and the rain forest of El Yunque. What they don't see is the man who spends his life making these things available to the tourist ... Miguel Domenech, the executive director of Puerto Rico Tourism. Let me be quite blunt about the following recipe. Miguel negotiated a deal with me. If I showed pictures of the great attractions of Puerto Rico in my report, all of which are really good to look at, then Miguel would show me his recipe for chicken and rice which is really good to eat. It's an excellent one pot meal.

4 tablespoons olive oil
One 3-pound frying chicken, cut into 8 pieces with skin removed
1 large onion, chopped
1 green bell pepper, ribs and seeds removed, chopped
2 tablespoons capers
$^{1}/_{4}$ cup small pimento stuffed olives
1 cup prepared tomato sauce
1 tablespoon dried oregano
1 teaspoon red pepper flakes
3 cloves garlic, minced
3 cups long grain rice
$4^{1}/_{2}$ cups chicken broth
$^{1}/_{2}$ cup chopped parsley
$^{1}/_{2}$ cup cooked peas
3 tablespoons chopped pimento

1. In a large stockpot or Dutch Oven large enough to hold all of the ingredients, heat the oil and brown the chicken on all sides. Cover and lower the heat to a simmer. Simmer about 15 minutes.

2. Add the onion and green pepper and cook 4 minutes. Add the capers, olives, tomato sauce, oregano, pepper flakes and garlic and cook for another 4 to 5 minutes.

3. Add the 3 cups of rice and stir the mixture well. Add the chicken broth and the parsley and stir. Cover the pot and reduce the heat to a simmer. Simmer for approximately 20 minutes or until the liquid is absorbed and the rice is tender.

4. Garnish with the peas and pimento and serve.

Makes 6 servings

ABOUT CHICKEN
The chicken as we know it today is a descendent of the red jungle bird of Southeast Asia. It was domesticated in India as early as 2,500 B.C.

Although chicken is inexpensive and plentiful today, it wasn't always so. From the late 1500's when King Francis IV of France hoped for a "chicken in every pot," chicken was confined to Sunday dinner. The advent of modern poultry-raising technology in the twentieth century made chicken popular and available.

Fresh chicken is very perishable. For best results, buy and cook chicken the same day, especially if it is cut up or split. Nutritionally, chicken can be a very good source of lean protein. Light meat is lower in fat and calories than dark meat and most of the fat and calories are in the skin. Take the skin off your chicken, even before you cook it, and you reduce the fat by more than half. Smaller broilers and fryers have less fat and calories than older birds such as roasters or stewing hens.

The mild taste of chicken meat can be greatly enhanced by the use of a marinade. There are two types of marinades—wet and dry. A wet marinade, originally developed as a brine for pickling, contains an acid such as lemon juice to tenderize the bird, and an oil to lubricate it. In India, chicken is marinated in yogurt and cardamom; Greeks use lemon juice, olive oil, garlic and oregano. Dry marinades are combinations of herbs and spices that are rubbed into the chicken skin with a little oil.

CHICKEN WITH PEACH SAUCE
JACKSONVILLE INN
JACKSONVILLE, OREGON

During the 1850's, gold was discovered near the town of Jacksonville, Oregon and the joint began to jump. Prospectors arrived from all over the world searching for wealth beyond their wildest dreams. The miners went up into the hills and used their pans to separate the gold from the earth. Then the cooks in Jacksonville used their pans to separate the gold from the miners. The old prospectors did not spend much effort cooking while they were searching for gold. They were therefore quite willing to spend big bucks for good food when they came into town. These days the good cooking takes place at the Jacksonville Inn and chef Diane Menzie is in charge of the mother lode, which takes the form of Chicken with Peach Sauce.

One 20-ounce bag frozen peaches (or 4 large fresh ones)
1 cup white wine (or chicken stock)
1 teaspoon cinnamon
$1/8$ cup sugar
$1/2$ cup flour
1 egg, beaten with 1 tablespoon water
$3/4$ cup hazelnuts (or pecans), finely chopped
2 tablespoons vegetable oil
2 chicken breasts, boned, skinned, split in half and slightly flattened

1. In a large skillet, place the peaches, white wine, cinnamon, and sugar and stir gently over medium heat until the peaches are tender and heated through. The sauce will reduce slightly and thicken. Set aside and keep warm.

2. Set up an assembly line: place the flour on a flat plate, the egg mixture in a large bowl, and the chopped nuts on a flat plate.

3. In a large skillet, heat the oil until it is hot.

4. Dip the chicken into the flour and shake off any excess. Then into the egg mixture and finally into the chopped nuts. Place the coated chicken into the skillet and saute over moderate heat for approximately **3** minutes on each side until completely cooked.

5. To serve, place half a chicken breast on a dinner plate and top with a portion of the peach sauce.

Makes 4 servings

GRILLED CHICKEN WITH YOGURT
HALCYON HOTEL
LONDON, ENGLAND

The Halcyon Hotel is a small and very elegant establishment in London, England. It was recently constructed inside two handsome private homes and each of the 44 suites has a unique style of decoration. A guest at the Halcyon gets the feeling that very rich friends have just invited you to spend a few days in their London residence. The hotel has an excellent kitchen, with a series of dishes that are low in fat and low in cholesterol, but high in good taste . . . just what you would expect from a rich friend. The following recipe from chef James Robinson is an example.

Marinade:
1 tablespoon fresh ginger, grated
1 teaspoon ground cardamom
1 teaspoon coriander
Juice of 1 lemon
1 tablespoon minced fresh mint
1 cup plain low-fat yogurt

Sauce:
$1/2$ cucumber, peeled, seeded and coarsely grated (about $1/3$ cup)
1 tablespoon chopped fresh mint
1 garlic clove, minced
Juice of $1/2$ lemon
1 cup plain low-fat yogurt
Salt and pepper to taste

3 chicken breasts, boned and skinned and cut in half (6 halves)
Fresh mint for garnish

1. In a baking dish mix all of the marinade ingredients. Place the chicken breasts in the marinade, turning once to coat both sides of the chicken. Cover and refrigerate for 24 hours.

2. In a small mixing bowl combine all of the sauce ingredients. Cover and chill until ready to use.

3. Grill chicken breasts until done, about 4 minutes per side. Place a generous serving of the sauce on each dinner plate, top with the chicken breast and garnish with a fresh sprig of mint. Serve at once.

Makes 6 servings

HOMEMADE YOGURT

2 cups milk
2 tablespoons plain low-fat yogurt

1. In a very clean saucepan, heat milk to 180° F. Then allow it to cool to 110° F.

2. Meanwhile, wash a glass jar with a tight-fitting lid in very hot soapy water. Rinse well with hot water.

3. Stir the store-bought yogurt into the milk. Pour the mixture into the glass jar and seal tight.

4. Put the jar into a preheated 100° F. oven or insulated picnic cooler for 7 hours. The longer the incubation, the more tangy the yogurt. (Once you refrigerate, the process stops.)

5. Refrigerate the yogurt for 2 hours before using. It will hold in the refrigerator for about 1 week. Save some of the yogurt from this batch to use as a starter for your next batch of yogurt.

Makes 2 cups

CHICKEN IN CITRUS SAUCE
RITZ HOTEL HEALTH CLUB
PARIS, FRANCE

This recipe was adapted from the menu of the health club at the Ritz Hotel in Paris. The kitchen is directed by Guy Legay, who is one of the leading chefs of France. The dishes are low in fat, low in sodium, low in calories, nutritionally well-balanced, and they look and taste great. For more Ritz Health Club recipes see pages 38, 40 and 41.

2 tablespoons vegetable oil
4 chicken breasts, skinless, boneless, split in half
3/4 cup low sodium chicken broth
1 small yellow onion, diced
3/4 cup orange juice
One 8-ounce can peaches packed in water or 1 fresh peach that
    has been boiled in water for 2 minutes and peeled
1 tablespoon distilled white vinegar
1 tablespoon honey
2 tablespoons plain low-fat yogurt
1 bunch broccoli flowerets
2 large carrots, in bite sized slices

1. In a large skillet, heat the oil over medium-high heat and sear the chicken for one minute on each side. Then add the chicken broth, reduce heat and simmer covered for 5 minutes. Remove the chicken from the pan and set aside.

3. Add the onion to the same pan and let stock reduce by half.

4. Add the orange juice, peaches, vinegar and honey. Simmer 5 minutes. Allow this mixture to cool to room temperature and add the yogurt.

5. Process this sauce in a blender or food processor until smooth.

6. Blanch the broccoli and carrots in boiling water until done but still crisp, about 4 minutes.

7. Cover the bottom of a warm serving dish with the citrus sauce. Slice the chicken breasts on an angle into 1/4-inch-thick slices. Arrange them in a circle just inside the outer border of the sauce. Repeat the process, arranging the carrots in a circle just inside the border of chicken. Arrange the broccoli flowerets in a mound in the center of the carrot circle. Serve warm.

Makes 8 servings

POULTRY TIPS

When storing raw poultry in the refrigerator, be sure that it is tightly wrapped, to prevent the meat or its juices from coming into contact with any other surfaces. Assume that all raw chicken has some salmonella bacteria that could cause food poisoning.

Wash raw chicken surfaces inside and out with cold water. Wash any surface that the raw poultry comes in contact with before it touches anything else. After you have touched raw poultry, wash your hands before you touch any other foods.

Make sure that the internal temperature of cooked poultry reaches at least 180° F. before serving. Never partially cook poultry.

Don't store poultry—cooked or raw—with stuffing inside. The densely packed stuffing stays warm and promotes bacterial growth. If you are going to hold stuffed chicken or other fowl for more than a few minutes, remove the stuffing after the bird is cooked and refrigerate it separately.

Advertisement for an oil cooking stove 1897

MEATS

ABOUT PORK

Pork is the meat of the pig, one of our oldest sources of meat. The wild boar is the pig's first ancestor, and some of the prehistoric cave paintings depict the wild boar hunt.

The first pork recipes stem from China, are dated about 500 B.C., and call for a suckling pig roasted in a pit. The Chinese and the Romans were adept at smoking and curing pork for use in the winter months. The tradition of slaughtering hogs for meat, sausages, ham and lard continues to this day. Among the Cajuns of southwest Louisiana it is a community event called *la boucherie*. The Spanish conquistador Hernando de Soto brought the first pigs to Florida in 1525. The majority of pigs in the United States are raised in Iowa, Illinois and Missouri.

Pork has become less fatty in recent years. A 3-ounce portion contains 200 calories, and 80 milligrams of cholesterol. Pork is a good source of B vitamins and minerals.

PORK LOIN WITH RICE
OLD SAN JUAN, PUERTO RICO

Jan D'Esopo studied art at Bennington College in Vermont and Yale University. Today she lives in Puerto Rico's Old San Juan. She paints, runs an art gallery and a wonderful little inn with ten rooms and a serious kitchen. When she sets a table it's decorated with sculpture and plated with dishes that are produced in the gallery. She demonstrated her culinary art skills with this recipe for Roast Pork with Rice.

1 cup wild rice
1 teaspoon salt
1 teaspoon black peppercorns
3 cloves garlic, chopped
1/4 cup chopped green olives
1/4 cup dark rum
One 3- to 4- pound pork loin, trimmed but with a layer of fat on top
2 tablespoons butter, or vegetable oil
3 jalapeño peppers, seeded, ribs removed and minced
1/2 cup chopped onion
1/2 cup chopped red bell pepper
3 tablespoons chopped cilantro or Chinese parsley
2 cups Basmati or whole grain rice
2 cubes chicken bouillon
3 drops of Tabasco, or more to taste
Chopped cilantro for garnish, optional

1. Preheat oven to 350° F.

2. In a small bowl, soak the wild rice in water for 30 minutes.

3. Using a mortar and pestle, or the bottom of a heavy pot, grind the salt and peppercorns together. Place the mixture into a bowl and add the garlic, green olives and dark rum to make a moist paste.

4. Place the loin, fat side down in a ovenproof roasting pan. Make a small "X", about 3/4 inch deep, with a sharp knife every 2 inches along the roast. Stuff the paste in the holes. Turn the roast over, with the fat side up. Make small diagonal slits in the meat about 3/4 inch deep and 2 inches apart. Insert the paste in the slits and smother the roast with the remaining paste. Place the pork in the oven and cook to an internal temperature of 160° F., for a medium-done roast, approximately 1 1/2 hours or 20 to 25 minutes per pound. Let stand 10 minutes before carving. Pour the pan drippings over the roast to serve.

5. In a large stockpot or saucepan with a tight-fitting lid, melt the butter. Add the jalapeños, onion, and red pepper and saute for 10 minutes. Add the cilantro and the Basmati rice. Stir until the rice is thoroughly coated with butter. Drain and rinse the wild rice and add it to the pot. Cover with water, approximately 5 to 6 cups. Add the bouillon and stir to dissolve. Add the Tabasco. Cover with a lid and cook over low heat for 50 to 55 minutes. Remove from heat and let stand, covered, 10 minutes longer. Garnish with chopped cilantro.

Makes 10 to 12 servings

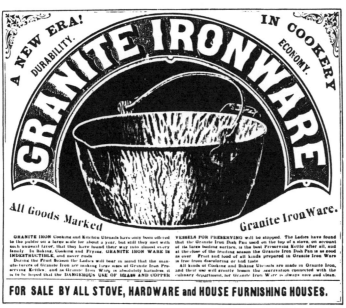

Cookware advertisement 1888

PORK MEDALLIONS
JACKSONVILLE INN
JACKSONVILLE, OREGON

When homesteaders first arrived in Oregon territory they were astonished by the abundant supply of wild nuts that were in the forest. There was also a massive variety of wild berries. When you have a forest filled with wild foods you have the perfect spot for raising pigs and within a few years Oregon farmers were producing some of the finest pork. They still do. The following sauteed pork loin recipe was prepared by chef Diane Menzie from the Jacksonville Inn. It's part of her low-fat menu and one of the Inn's most popular dishes.

4 tablespoons flour

1 1/2 pounds pork tenderloin, trimmed and cut into 1/2-inch thick medallions

2 tablespoons vegetable oil

2 cups sliced fresh mushrooms

1 tablespoon fresh rosemary or 1 teaspoon dried rosemary, chopped

1 shallot, minced (or 2 tablespoons minced onion)

Freshly ground black pepper to taste

1/2 cup beef broth

1/3 cup dry Marsala wine, or additional beef broth

Chopped parsley for garnish

1. Put the flour in a shallow baking dish and lightly dredge the medallions in it.

2. In a large saute pan, heat the oil. Place the medallions in the pan and cook 4 minutes on each side.

3. Add the mushrooms, rosemary, shallot and freshly ground black pepper to the saute pan. Cook for 3 minutes. Add the beef broth and boil rapidly, until only 2 to 3 tablespoons remain. Add the Marsala and cook 8 to 10 minutes more.

4. Serve the meat with the sauce poured over it and garnish with chopped parsley.

Makes 4 servings

JARLSBERG STUFFED PEPPERS
GRAND HOTEL ♦ OSLO, NORWAY

The natural beauty of Norway is magnificent. High mountains. Deep valleys and thousands of miles of coast line that bring up the warm currents of the Gulf Stream and give the area a much more favorable temperature range than you might expect. The result of these unusual environmental conditions is a group of grasslands where cows thrive in clean, clear, pastures. For centuries the farmers of Norway have used their pure milk from these herds to make cheese. Their most famous is the semi-soft, part skim milk Jarlsberg. Jarlsberg is rather low in cholesterol and sodium but high in taste. The following recipe blends Jarlsberg cheese and beef together in a way that suggests a cheeseburger in a pepper.

4 large green, yellow or red bell peppers
Rock salt (optional)
1 pound lean ground beef
1 teaspoon Tabasco, or more to taste
2 cloves garlic, minced
$^1/_2$ teaspoon salt
$^1/_2$ teaspoon freshly ground black pepper
$^1/_4$ cup fresh lemon juice
3 slices whole wheat bread, toasted and pulled into very small pieces
1 $^1/_4$ cups Jarlsberg cheese, diced into $^1/_4$-inch cubes

1. Preheat oven to 350° F.

2. Stand peppers on their base and core from the top by removing the stem, ribs and seeds. Place them on a baking sheet on a bed of rock salt. The rock salt is used only to keep the peppers standing upright.

3. In a medium bowl, combine the beef, Tabasco, garlic, salt, pepper, and lemon juice. Mix well. Add the bread pieces and cheese.

4. Stuff the beef mixture loosely into the peppers.

5. Bake for 35 to 45 minutes, depending on the size of the peppers.

Makes 4 servings

HAM AND CHEESE PIE
RED ROOF INN ♦ PORTAGE LA PRAIRIE
MANITOBA, CANADA

The Red Roof Inn stands in Portage La Prairie, just outside of Winnipeg in the Canadian province of Manitoba. The building was constructed from a set of plans developed by the famous architect, Frank Lloyd Wright. The Inn is described as a bed and breakfast establishment but the place is very special. The beds have been slept in by people like Carole Lombard and Clark Gable and the breakfast menu features, dishes like snails, exotic fruits, homemade jams and strawberry champagne. It's owned and operated by Don and Donnee Pelechaty who have made each room into a museum of memorabilia. In addition to bed and breakfast accommodations, they host dinner parties, pre-nuptial dinners, weddings and wakes. One of their gastronomic specialities is the following ham and cheese pie.

Pastry for an 11-inch double pie crust
2 tablespoons butter
1 medium onion, chopped
2 cloves garlic, minced
2 1/2 cups chopped spinach, cooked and drained
5 eggs, (divided as below)
A grating of fresh nutmeg, optional
1/2 pound prosciutto or dry smoked ham, sliced
12 ounces mozzarella, sliced
Two 4-ounce jars of pimientos, drained

1. Preheat oven to 400° F. Grease an 11-inch deep dish pie pan.

2. Roll out 2/3 of the pastry and place it in the prepared pan allowing the pastry to overhang a little.

3. In a medium saute pan, melt the butter. Add the onion and garlic and saute until translucent, about 3 minutes. Add the spinach and cook 1 minute more. Set aside.

4. In a small bowl, whisk 4 of the eggs.

5. Grate the nutmeg over the pastry. Place half the prosciutto on the pastry. Pour a little of the egg on this layer. Follow by adding half the cheese, half the spinach and half the pimiento, pouring some of the egg between each layer. Repeat the layers and pour any remaining egg over the top.

6. Roll out the remaining pastry and cover the pie, sealing the edges. Make a small hole in the center of the pastry for steam to escape.

7. In a small bowl, combine the remaining egg with 1 tablespoon of water and whisk. Brush the surface of the pie with the egg wash.

8. Bake for 50 minutes. Let cool for 30 minutes before removing from pan. Serve warm.

Makes 6 servings

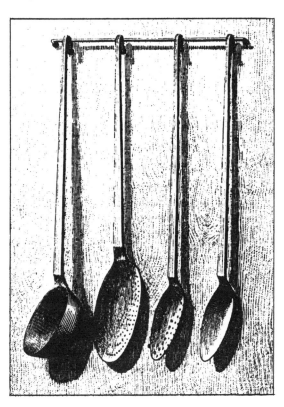

RINGNES BURGERS
FRAM MUSEUM
OSLO, NORWAY

Just outside the city of Oslo, Norway is a museum containing the ship that was used for a number of explorations to both the north and south poles. The name of the vessel is Fram *which means "forward."*

Explorations are very expensive and are always funded by a sponsor. Columbus had Queen Isabella, Lewis & Clark, who mapped most of the American northwest, were funded by a company that made fur hats, and the Norwegians were supported by the brewers of Ringnes beer. Of course, there were a few cases of Ringnes on board the Fram and the cook often put them to good use in his recipes. My favorite is his Ringnes Burgers.

2 tablespoons vegetable oil, (divided as follows)
1 medium onion, chopped
1/4 cup chopped pickled beets
1/4 cup chopped pickles
1 tablespoon capers, chopped
2 pounds ground beef
2 eggs
1/2 teaspoon salt
1/4 teaspoon freshly ground pepper
3/4 teaspoon chili powder
12 ounces of Ringnes or your favorite beer (divided as follows)

1. In a medium saute pan, heat 1 tablespoon of the vegetable oil. Add the onion and saute until it begins to turn golden, approximately 8 minutes. Add the beets, pickles, and capers and saute for 3 minutes.

2. In a medium bowl, combine the vegetable mixture with the beef, eggs, salt, pepper, chili powder and 1/4 cup of the beer. Mix well. Firmly shape the meat into six patties.

3. In a large saute pan, heat the remaining tablespoon of vegetable oil. Pan fry the patties until cooked to taste, approximately 6 to 7 minutes on each side for a medium burger. Remove the patties from the pan and set aside.

4. Pour off the grease from the saute pan. Add the remaining beer and cook for approximately 10 minutes, scraping up the brown bits with a spoon.

5. Pour the beer sauce over the burgers and serve.

Makes 6 servings

ABOUT HAMBURGERS

Along with hot dogs, hamburgers are the most American of all foods. The name hamburger is derived from the German port city of Hamburg, but that's not where hamburgers were born. Through the latter half of the nineteenth century, some form of hammered beef steak was served in restaurants there. But the first time the name hamburger was used was at the Louisiana Purchase Exposition and World's Fair in St. Louis in 1904.

The advent of the White Castle hamburger chain in the 1920's and the McDonald's chain in the 1950's spread hamburger culture deep into America.

Hamburgers should be called beef burgers because it is rare that hamburgers are made of veal, lamb or pork. Hamburger meat bought at the supermarket cannot contain more than 30 percent fat. A hamburger should contain 20 to 25 percent fat, although it is possible to buy meat that is as lean as 10 percent fat. Ground chuck has the proper fat content and the beefiest flavor.

STUFFED STEAK
NICK'S ITALIAN CAFE
McMINNVILLE, OREGON

Nick Peirano's restaurant has been described as an unofficial "club" for the winemakers of Oregon. Friendly, informal, moderate prices, the type of eatery that everyone would like to have in their neighborhood. This recipe was adapted from Nick's menu, it makes a simple club steak into a festive dish.

4 club steaks, 1-inch thick
1/4 cup basil, chopped
1/4 cup parsley, chopped
2 cloves of garlic, minced
1/4 cup grated Parmesan cheese
1/4 cup walnuts, finely chopped
1/4 pound sliced prosciutto or dry smoked ham
4 slices Muenster cheese
1 tablespoon olive oil
1/2 cup dry Marsala wine or beef stock

1. Place the steaks on a cutting board and slice horizontally through the center thickness of one side almost through to the other side. Unfold the meat into a butterfly shape, interior portion facing up. Pound with mallet or heavy pan to 1/4-inch thickness. Repeat on the remaining steaks.

2. In a small bowl, mix together the basil, parsley, garlic, Parmesan, and walnuts. Spread this mixture thinly on both interior sides of all 4 steaks.

3. On one side of the steak, place 1 slice of prosciutto or dry smoked ham, top with one slice of cheese. Fold the other side of the meat onto the cheese and prosciutto and press closed. Repeat with the remaining steaks.

4. Heat the olive oil in a large saute pan. Add the stuffed steaks to the pan and cook to desired doneness, 3 to 4 minutes per side for medium. Turn each steak once. Remove from saute pan to a serving platter.

5. Pour off any grease from the saute pan and add the Marsala or beef stock. Bring to a boil for 3 to 4 minutes, scraping up the brown bits in the saute pan.

Makes 4 servings

Advertisement for a rangetop charcoal broiler 1891

CURRIED VEAL
BANBURY HOUSE INN
SASKATCHEWAN, CANADA

The Banbury House Inn, in Wolseley, Saskatchewan, Canada, was once the private residence of a local lumber baron. In 1985 it was about to be demolished for a new housing development when it was saved by a chef named Ernest Boehm. He bought the house and moved it to its present site where it has become a splendid little Inn. The first settlers into the area of Wolseley were English and French. They were followed by settlers from Germany, Russia and Poland. The latest immigrants have brought in families from India and the Orient. The influence of the Indians is illustrated in Ernest's recipe for his Banbury Curried Veal.

2 tablespoons unsalted butter
1 medium onion, chopped
1 large clove garlic, minced
3 tablespoons curry powder
1/2 cup chopped celery
2 tablespoons cucumber, peeled and diced
2 tablespoons pimiento, chopped
2 large carrots, chopped
2 cups chicken stock
1/2 cup coconut milk
1 1/2 pounds veal scallopini
1/4 teaspoon salt
1/4 teaspoon freshly ground black pepper
4 tablespoons flour
2 tablespoons vegetable oil
3 cups prepared Basmati or whole grain rice
Chopped parsley to garnish, optional

1. In a large saucepan, melt the butter over moderate heat. Add the onion and garlic and saute until the onion is limp, approximately 3 minutes. Stir in the curry powder and cook for 2 more minutes.

2. Add the celery and stir. Add the cucumber, pimiento and carrots and cook for 1 minute. Add the chicken stock and bring to a boil. Cook for 5 minutes.

3. Puree the curry sauce in a food mill, food processor or blender and return the sauce to the pan. Stir in the coconut milk and reheat over low heat.

4. Cut the veal into 1/2-inch strips lengthwise.

5. In a shallow dish, combine the salt, pepper and flour. Roll the strips of veal in the seasoned flour until coated.

6. In a large saute pan, heat the oil. Add the veal and stir-fry 4 to 5 minutes. Remove the meat and reserve.

7. Serve veal on a bed of rice with the sauce poured on top. Garnish with the chopped parsley.

Makes 6 servings

ABOUT VEAL

Veal is baby beef. It is more common in Europe than in America, but in cities with large Italian populations veal is readily available. European farmers do not have as much pasture and crop land as American farmers do, so they often slaughter young beef animals when they are 2 to 5 months. old. They have been milk-fed their entire lives and have not had a chance to start exercising their muscles, which makes the meat creamy white and very tender. Some American veal is allowed to become a few months older and feed on grass. This veal is called calf.

Veal cutlets are thin, boneless pieces of meat cut from the rump or round portion of the animal. The best cutlets, called scaloppine, are cut across the grain from the single muscle of the top round. You may also come across cutlets that are cut from the whole hind leg that contain a small round bone in the center. This is a less successful cut.

PEPPER STEAK
WOLSELEY, SASKATCHEWAN, CANADA

Ernest Boehm is a missionary and he is working hard to spread his beliefs ... to convert the hearts and minds of the people around him. Ernest is a classic European chef and his mission is to bring top quality cooking to a very small town in the province of Saskatchewan, Canada. For many years he did his cooking in Switzerland but his wife's desire to be with her family brought them to the town of Wolseley. Ernest set-up an authentic French restaurant and socked it to 'em and the local residents quickly congregated. The theme of the following recipe is "the goodness of steak when joined with a heavenly pepper sauce."

4 boneless shell steaks
Salt and freshly ground black pepper
1 teaspoon white peppercorns
1 teaspoon black peppercorns
1 tablespoon vegetable oil
1/3 cup Cognac or beef stock
1/2 cup heavy cream
Chopped parsley for garnish

1. Season steaks with salt and pepper to taste.

2. With a mallet or heavy pan, crush the white and black peppercorns together.

3. In a large saute pan, heat the vegetable oil. Add the steaks and cook 5 to 6 minutes on each side for a medium steak. Remove the steaks from the saute pan.

4. Pour off most of the grease from the saute pan and add the peppercorns. Cook over medium heat for 30 seconds. Remove the saute pan from the heat and add the cognac. Return to medium heat and flame very carefully until the alcohol burns off. (If using the beef stock, it will not flame.) Cook for 3 to 4 minutes until thickened. Add the cream and boil until thickened, approximately 1 to 2 minutes. Return the steaks to the saute pan and turn once to coat. Remove to serving platter and pour the sauce over the steaks. Garnish with chopped parsley.

Makes 4 servings

ABOUT STEAK

Steak is a common word for a slice of meat; it almost always refers to beef and is usually cut against the grain.

The tendered cuts of steak—rib eye, T-bone, porterhouse, Delmonico, and others—can be broiled or pan-fried. Chuck, arm and round steaks all need to be either marinated or cooked in liquid to be tender. The flank is just under the tenderloin, and contains one of the versatile cuts, the flank steak. The most common flank steak dish is London broil.

USDA prime, choice and select are the three main gradings for steak. The gradings are based on the quality of fat or "marbling" in the meat. Ninety percent of the steak we eat is choice. Prime is very expensive and hard to come by and nearly all of it is bought by and served in restaurants. Select is the leanest grade of steak and is now being upgraded by the beef industry. Steak, like all beef, is a good source of protein, iron and B vitamins.

RITZY BEEF
RITZ HOTEL
PARIS, FRANCE

The Ritz Hotel in Paris opened in 1898, and from the very beginning it was famous for its food which was prepared under the direction of the great chef Auguste Escoffier. One of the major reasons for the long history of success is the organizational structure of the kitchen which was originally put into place during the late 1800's by Escoffier. He set-up the kitchen in five main areas. The garde-manger *prepared all the basic ingredients for the entire kitchen. No matter what a chef is preparing, the uncooked elements, fruits, vegetables, meat, fish, poultry, butter, eggs; it comes from the* garde-manger. *Next is the* rotisseur, *who handles the roasting, grilling, sauteing and deep frying. The* entremetier *directs the production of soups, vegetables and desserts. The* patissier *covers all the pastry, both those that are for the sweets like a tart, or for a savory like a chicken pot pie. Finally, there are the sauce makers. The head chef receives an order from the dining room and each area does its thing ... bringing all the elements together for the final assembly under the eye of the master. The following recipe uses the kitchen staff according to Escoffier's plan.*

4 filet mignons, cut 1-inch thick
Salt and freshly ground black pepper
4 tablespoons butter (divided as below)
1 shallot, minced
2 cups fresh mushrooms, quartered
1/2 cup beef broth
1/3 cup Madeira, or additional beef broth
Chopped parsley for garnish, optional

1. Season the beef with salt and pepper to taste.

2. In a medium saute pan, melt 2 tablespoons of the butter. When the butter stops foaming, saute the filets for 6 to 7 minutes on each side, for a medium rare steak. Remove the meat from the pan and pour off any grease.

3. In a small saute pan, melt the remaining butter. Saute the shallot for 2 minutes. Add the mushrooms and cook for 3 minutes until lightly browned. Set aside.

4. In the meat pan, add the broth and boil rapidly, scraping up the browned bits, until 2 tablespoons remain. Add the Madeira and boil rapidly until the sauce thickens, approximately 2 to 3 minutes. Add the mushrooms back in and simmer for 1 minute more.

5. Serve the steaks with the sauce over the top and garnish with parsley, if desired.

Makes 4 servings

ABOUT SHALLOTS

Shallots are the high-class European cousin of the onion; they are shaped like garlic cloves and grow in clusters like garlic. Their flavor is distinctive—tangier than red onions but not as sharp as garlic.

Shallots are used extensively in French cooking. They are native to the Middle East and were brought to Europe by returning Crusaders. French explorers brought them to America. When buying shallots, look for bulbs that are about 3/4 inch in diameter. The skin should be smooth and dry.

PASTA & RICE

SANDS PASTA
SANDS HOTEL & CASINO
SAN JUAN, PUERTO RICO

The Sands Hotel & Casino in San Juan, Puerto Rico is well known for its party atmosphere and this recipe will help them develop a reputation for Party Pasta. The preparation is very simple and very fast.

2 tablespoons olive oil
4 cloves garlic, minced
2 cups freshly chopped tomatoes
One 10-ounce package frozen artichoke hearts (or canned, cut
    into bite sized pieces)
1/4 cup fresh chopped basil
1 teaspoon rosemary, crushed
1 1/2 teaspoons fresh thyme (or 3/4 teaspoon dried)
3/4 pound linguini, cooked
Salt and freshly ground black pepper
4 tablespoons grated Pecorino Romano cheese

1. In a large skillet, heat the oil and saute the garlic over medium-high heat for about 2 minutes.

2. Add the chopped tomatoes and the artichoke hearts and cook for another 2 to 3 minutes. Add the basil and other herbs and cook for another 2 to 3 minutes.

3. Toss in the linguini and mix gently until all of the ingredients are well combined. Season with salt and pepper to taste.

4. Just before serving, toss with the Pecorino Romano cheese.

Makes 4 servings

PECORINO ROMANO CHEESE

The ancient Romans made dozens of different cheeses and records clearly show that they used many of them as cooking ingredients. Pecorino Romano cheese was a regular part of the diet of the Roman legions. The soldiers carried the cheese with them as a convenient source of energy and inspiration. Italy soon became the center of cheesemaking.

Today, Pecorino Romano is produced in Sardinia. It is a hard grained cheese made entirely of fresh sheep milk. It is firm enough to grate and yet soft enough to cut in slivers. The production of Pecorino Romano starts with the gathering of the sheep herd and the milking. The milk is processed in modern Pecorino Romano facilities. When the milk reaches the plant it is placed in containers and heated. Negative bacteria is destroyed while at the same time those microorganisms essential to the making of the cheese are allowed to flourish. A starter enzyme is introduced into the milk and a short time later, the rennet is added. The entire process is monitored by a complex computer system. The solid curds are allowed to form, after which they are broken up into small pieces. The liquid whey is then pressed out. The cheese is cut into large rectangular blocks and placed into perforated stainless steel molds. Weights are set on the top, to press out additional whey and pressure the curds into their traditional form. The cheeses are then removed from the steel containers and wrapped in a flexible form which contains the seal of the authentic Pecorino Romano maker. It is the symbolic head of a sheep with the words *Pecorino Romano* underneath. This emblem is pressed into the surface of every cheese and signals to the consumer that the product being purchased is authentic Pecorino Romano.

Once the cheese has been removed from the mold, it goes into the ripening cellar for a six to eight month period. Each of the cheeses can weigh up to 70 pounds. Eighty percent of the Pecorino Romano produced in Italy is consumed by people in the United States. It is used primarily as an ingredient in cooking or as a grating cheese at the table. It supplies taste, texture and valuable nutrients.

CHICKEN, PASTA AND PECORINO ROMANO
HEATHMAN HOTEL
PORTLAND, OREGON

The Heathman Hotel in Portland, Oregon is an example of how a hotel can be almost completely directed towards making each guest feel totally at home. The General Manager of the hotel is Mary Arnstad, and her Executive Chef, George Tate and Chef/Manager, Greg Higgins make the Heathman a real treat. The following recipe is part of their standard menu and makes a fine main dish.

$^1/_4$ cup olive oil
$^1/_4$ cup peas, fresh or frozen
$^1/_4$ cup mushrooms, sliced
1 cup chicken breast, cut into bite sized pieces
$^1/_4$ cup roughly chopped spinach
$^1/_4$ cup roughly chopped basil
$^1/_8$ cup chopped prosciutto (or ham)
$^1/_4$ cup white wine (or chicken broth)
$^1/_2$ cup chicken broth
4 cups fettucini, cooked
4 tablespoons grated Pecorino Romano cheese
4 tablespoons hazelnuts (or walnuts), chopped

1. In a large skillet, heat the oil and add the peas. Cook for 2 minutes. Add the mushrooms and cook for 2 minutes. Add the chicken and cook for 2 more minutes.

2. Add the spinach and basil and cook for 1 minute. Add the prosciutto and cook 2 more minutes. Add the wine and chicken broth and cook for 3 minutes until mixture is slightly reduced.

3. Add the fettucini and cook for 3 minutes, until it is heated through.

4. Remove the pan from the heat and stir in the Pecorino Romano cheese.

5. Transfer the pasta to a serving dish and sprinkle with the chopped nuts.

Makes 4 servings

PORTLAND PESTO PASTA
HEATHMAN HOTEL
PORTLAND, OREGON

Portland's Heathman Hotel was originally built in 1927. In 1984, it was renovated at a cost of $16 million. Located in the heart of the downtown commercial and cultural district, the hotel takes great pride in its restaurant's seasonal menus.

2 tablespoons olive oil
$^1/_2$ cup sliced mushrooms
$^1/_2$ cup fresh spinach
$^1/_4$ cup basil leaves,whole
$^1/_2$ cup heavy cream
$^3/_4$ pound linguini, cooked
4 tablespoons pesto sauce (recipe follows)
Salt and freshly ground black pepper
4 tablespoons grated Pecorino Romano cheese

1. In a large skillet over medium-high heat, saute the mushrooms in the olive oil until slightly browned, about 3 minutes. Add the spinach and the whole basil leaves and cook for another 2 minutes until the greens have barely wilted.

2. Add the heavy cream and bring the mixture to a strong simmer. Add the pasta and toss gently until the ingredients are combined and the pasta is heated through, about 3 minutes.

3. Swirl the pesto sauce into the mixture and cook only for another 2 minutes to make sure the pasta is hot.

4. Put the mixture in a serving dish and toss with the Pecorino Romano cheese.

Makes 4 servings

PESTO SAUCE

$1/2$ **cup closely packed basil leaves**
4 garlic cloves
$1/4$ **cup olive oil**
$1/4$ **cup pine nuts, or walnuts**

1. Place the basil leaves in a food processor.

2. With the machine running, add the garlic through the feed tube and process until the mixture is finely minced.

3. With the machine still running, slowly add the oil through the feed tube and continue processing until you have a thick and creamy mixture.

4. Add the nuts and process another minute until they are finely chopped. Use as directed.

Makes about 3/4 cup

NOTE: Chef George Tate presents this dish by placing a portion of your favorite marinara sauce on each plate and serving the pasta on top garnished with a sprig of fresh basil.

PAELLA
CONDADO PLAZA HOTEL & CASINO
SAN JUAN, PUERTO RICO

The word paella *originally referred to a pan, a* paellera, *which comes from the Latin word for pan,* patella. *Today paella has come to mean a rice, chicken and seafood dish that probably originated in the Spanish province of Valencia. The following recipe was adapted from a Le Lo Lai Festival in San Juan, Puerto Rico. It is truly a one-pot meal. For other recipes from the Le Lo Lai Festival, see pages 26 and 125.*

1/4 cup olive oil
4 chicken breasts, bone in, skin off
1/2 pound chorizo or other sausage, cut in bite sized pieces
2 medium onions, chopped
2 large red bell peppers, seeds and ribs removed, chopped
3 cups uncooked white rice
2 tablespoons parsley, dried
4 garlic cloves, minced
1 Bay leaf
6 cups chicken broth
2 tablespoons turmeric (or 1/2 teaspoon saffron threads in 2 tablespoons of water)
8 large shrimp, cleaned and deveined
8 little neck clams, scrubbed
8 mussels, scrubbed and debearded

1. In a large Dutch oven or flame-proof casserole, heat the olive oil over medium-high heat. Add the chicken and saute until well browned. Remove and set aside.

2. Add the sausages to the oil and brown on all sides. Set aside with the chicken.

3. To the pot, add the onions and peppers and saute until the onions are wilted, about 3 minutes.

4. Add the rice and stir until the rice is well coated with the oil. Add the parsley, garlic and the Bay leaf and stir well to combine.

5. Add the chicken broth and the turmeric and stir again. Bury the chicken and the sausage in the rice mixture. Let the mixture cook, uncovered, for 10 minutes.

6. Add the shrimp and the shellfish, placing them as deep into the rice mixture as they will go, cover and simmer slowly, over low heat, for another 15 minutes.

7. Remove the cover and simmer for another 6 minutes until most of the liquid is absorbed and the rice is tender.

8. Remove and discard the Bay leaf and arrange paella in a serving dish.

Makes 4 to 6 servings

SPINACH & RICOTTA LASAGNA
NICK'S ITALIAN CAFE
McMINNVILLE, OREGON

For another recipe from Nick's Italian Cafe see the Stuffed Steak recipe on page 68.

4 tablespoons butter or margarine
1 small onion, chopped
4 tablespoons flour
3 cups skim milk
$^1/_2$ teaspoon nutmeg
Salt and freshly ground white pepper
1 pound low-fat ricotta cheese
$^1/_2$ pound fresh mushrooms, cleaned and sliced
1 pound fresh spinach
6 medium tomatoes, chopped
1 pound lasagna noodles, cooked and rinsed under cold water
8 ounces skim milk mozzarella, grated

1. In a large, heavy saucepan, over medium-high heat, melt the butter or margarine and saute the onion just until wilted, about 2 minutes. Lower the heat and add the flour, stirring constantly so that the mixture does not scorch. Cook for about 3 minutes.

2. Pour the skim milk into the saucepan and whisk constantly until the mixture thickens, about 6 minutes. Season with the nutmeg, salt and pepper to taste. Remove the pan from the heat and cool for 10 minutes. Add the ricotta cheese and stir until well-incorporated. Set aside.

3. In a non-stick skillet over medium-high heat, saute the mushrooms for approximately 3 minutes, until slightly browned. Add the spinach and stir until wilted, about 2 minutes. Remove the pan from the heat and stir in the chopped tomatoes Set aside.

4. Preheat the oven to 450° F.

5. In a baking dish, place a small amount of the ricotta mixture, just to coat the bottom of the pan. Then proceed by layering in the following manner: a layer of noodles, a portion of the ricotta mixture, some of the vegetables, and a sprinkling of the mozzarella cheese. Continue to layer the ingredients this way until the top layer of noodles. This is covered only with a portion of the ricotta mixture and some of the mozzarella so that the lasagna has a nice white top layer. (This can be prepared a day ahead up to this point and held, tightly covered, in the refrigerator.)

6. Place the baking dish, uncovered, in the oven for approximately 30 minutes, until the mixture is heated through and the top is slightly golden. (If you have made the lasagna earlier and it has been refrigerated, bring it to room temperature before heating.) Serve.

Makes 8 to 10 servings

NOTE: Whenever you want to pre-cook pasta for future use, you can prevent the pasta from sticking together quite easily. After the noodles have been cooked, thoroughly, drain them and run them under cold water until they can be handled easily. Transfer the pasta to a large bowl and toss with 1 to 2 tablespoons of olive oil. Toss the mixture to make sure that all of the noodles are well coated and set the dish aside until you need it.

ABOUT RICOTTA CHEESE
Ricotta cheese is a fresh cheese similar to cottage cheese. It has a very mild flavor and delicate consistency, and heats well in dishes like lasagna. It is made from whey or buttermilk,, and comes in regular and part-skim varieties. At 4 and 2 percent fat, they are both extremely low-fat cheeses, and are recommended in low-fat diets.

Ricotta is a healthy substitute for sour cream in some recipes.

VEGETABLES

LAYERED IDAHO POTATOES
DUCK'S AMERICAN BAR & GRILL
BOISE, IDAHO

Duck's American Bar & Grill in Boise, Idaho is an informal eatery with a relaxed atmosphere. Things just flow together for the pleasure of patrons. The following recipe expresses this approach, the ingredients slide into each other and into the oven. The finished dish makes an excellent vegetable course for almost any meal.

2 Idaho potatoes, partially cooked and thinly sliced
1 small eggplant, sliced into thin rounds and sauteed in a little vegetable oil
1/2 cup fresh basil leaves or 1 teaspoon dried
One 4-ounce log goat cheese
1 medium tomato, thinly sliced
1/4 cup sun-dried tomatoes in olive oil, cut into strips
1 teaspoon fresh thyme or 1/2 teaspoon dried
2 tablespoons capers

1. Pre-heat the oven to 350° F. Lightly oil a 9- x 9-inch baking dish.

2. Layer the ingredients into the baking dish in the following manner: half of the potatoes, the eggplant, half of the basil, half of the goat cheese, the remaining potatoes, the fresh tomato, the sun-dried tomatoes, the remaining basil, thyme and capers. Top with the remaining goat cheese and bake, uncovered, until the potatoes can be easily pierced with a knife, about 35 minutes.

Makes 4 servings

SPECIAL SOIL FOR A SPECIAL POTATO
THE IDAHO RUSSET AND HOW TO BAKE IT

The geological history of Idaho has given it a fascinating collection of surface features. Idaho has more than 200 mountains that go up over 8,000 feet. Ancient glacial ice formed lakes and seas which deposited valuable layers of sediment in the soil. River systems carved a web of canyons, including North America's deepest gorge, and lava flows have covered the surface.

Interesting information for a geologist or a tourist, but what has all that geography have to do with cooking? Well ... quite frankly, everything if you love potatoes like I do. The volcanic soil, the abundance of clean water and the fresh mountain air have created the perfect environment for growing what is probably the world's most famous potato ... the Idaho Russet. And the perfect way to bake it is very simple.

1. Scrub the potato and dry it.

2. Prick it a few times with a fork, which will allow the steam to escape. That will give you a dry and fluffy texture.

3. Don't wrap it in foil. The foil will steam the potato.

4. Bake the potato in a preheated 400° F. oven for 1 hour. The internal temperature will be about 210° F. You will have a dark, crispy skin and fluffy interior.

LEMONY IDAHO POTATOES

These potatoes are easy to prepare and have a light and refreshing flavor. The taste of the lemon combines perfectly with the oregano.

2 pounds Idaho potatoes
¹/₄ cup olive oil
The juice of 1 lemon plus the grated zest
Salt and freshly ground black pepper
2 teaspoons dried oregano

1. Peel the potatoes, if desired. Cut them into 2-inch pieces. Cook the potatoes in plenty of boiling water until just tender. They must not overcook or they will be watery. Drain and return to a saucepan.

2. Over moderate heat, shake the saucepan with the potatoes to dry them out completely. Place them into a heated serving dish and keep warm.

3. While the potatoes are cooking, combine the other ingredients and beat until creamy. Pour over the potatoes, making sure to coat the slices well. Serve warm at room temperature or chilled.

Makes 4 servings

TWICE-BAKED IDAHO POTATOES WITH CHEDDAR TOPPING

Roy Reed is the Chairman of the Idaho Potato Commission. He and his wife Larene work a 365 acre farm producing some of the world's finest potatoes. These potatoes make a fine side dish for any meat, fish or poultry. They are, with the addition of a salad, sufficiently substantial to make a light lunch.

4 large Idaho potatoes, washed, and poked a few times on each side with the tines of a fork.

Topping:
1 cup shredded Cheddar cheese
$^1/_2$ cup light sour cream, or plain low-fat yogurt
$^1/_4$ cup margarine, softened
4 scallions, chopped

1. Pre-heat the oven to 375° F.

2. Place the potatoes on the oven rack and bake until fork tender, about 1 hour. Let the potatoes cool until they can be handled. Do not turn off the oven.

3. In a medium bowl, combine all of the ingredients except the potatoes. Mix well and set aside until just before serving.

4. Cut a $^1/_2$-inch slice off one side of each potato. Leaving a $^1/_2$-inch border around the insides and bottom of the potatoes, scoop out the flesh and mix with the prepared topping, thoroughly combining the ingredients and eliminating most of the lumps. Spoon the mixture back into the potato shells.

5. Place the potatoes on a baking dish or a cookie sheet and bake for 15 to 20 minutes, until golden brown.

Serves 4

GERMAN-STYLE IDAHO POTATO SALAD

2 pounds Idaho potatoes
1/8 cup vegetable oil
3 tablespoons cider vinegar
3/4 cup beef broth
1 small onion, finely minced
Salt and freshly ground black pepper
1/4 cup freshly chopped parsley

1. Place the potatoes in a large saucepan and cover them with water. Cook over medium heat until tender. Remove the potatoes from the water and cool for 10 minutes, until easy to handle. Cut them into slices about 1/4 to 1/2 inch thick.

2. Place the potatoes in a large shallow bowl and sprinkle with oil and vinegar. Add the broth and the onion. Season with salt and pepper to taste. Toss the mixture gently.

3. Cover the bowl and let the mixture stand at room temperature for 2 1/2 hours, tossing gently after 1 hour. This salad should not be chilled. Just before serving, garnish with parsley.

Makes 4 servings

THE EXCELLENT NUTRITION
OF THE IDAHO POTATO

In 1836, a missionary named Henry Harmon Spalding planted the first potato in the state of Idaho. He wanted to show the local Indians that they could provide nutritious foods for themselves through agriculture as well as by hunting and gathering. Henry could not have selected a better food to make his point. The potato that comes out the rich volcanic soil of Idaho is a nutritional gold mine. It contains protein, iron, thiamine, niacin, potassium and vitamin C. A five-ounce baked potato has only 100 calories. It contains 24 grams of complex carbohydrates and is almost fat-free. There are only 4 milligrams. of sodium in five ounces of baked potato, which makes it virtually sodium-free.

I can't think of a food that does a better job of meeting today's criteria for a healthful diet. Low in calories, almost no fat, almost no sodium, high in complex carbohydrates and packed with valuable vitamins and minerals. The potato farmers in Idaho have spent over 100 years collecting great potato recipes. The following are a few examples.

OVEN-FRIED GARLIC POTATOES

4 Idaho potatoes, thinly sliced
2 tablespoons olive oil
4 garlic cloves, minced
2 teaspoons crushed rosemary

1. Pre-heat the oven to 375° F.

2. In a large bowl, toss all of the ingredients together, coating the potatoes evenly.

3. Pour the mixture into a baking dish and bake, uncovered, until the potatoes can be easily pierced with a knife and are golden brown and crisp on the top, about 45 minutes.

Makes 4 servings

RICOTTA-STUFFED POTATO BOATS

4 Idaho potatoes, scrubbed clean, and poked a few times on each side with the tines of a fork
¹/₄ cup minced onion
4 cloves of garlic, minced
¹/₂ pound low-fat ricotta cheese
¹/₄ cup low-fat sour cream, or plain low-fat yogurt
¹/₄ cup fresh basil, chopped
1 bell pepper, chopped
4 teaspoons Parmesan cheese

1. Pre-heat the oven to 375° F. Place the potatoes on the oven rack and bake until fork tender, about 1 hour. Set aside until they cool to a point where they are easy to handle.

2. In a small, non-stick skillet, saute the onions with the garlic until barely browned.

3. In a large bowl, combine the onions and garlic with the ricotta, sour cream, basil and bell pepper. Stir until blended.

4. Cut a ¹/₂-inch slice off one side of each potato. Leaving a ¹/₂-inch wall on the inside and bottom of the potato, scoop out the flesh of the potato. Add the potato flesh to the bowl with the other ingredients. Mix well, eliminating most of the lumps.

5. Fill the potato boats with the potato-cheese mixture and place on a baking tray or cookie sheet. Top each with 1 teaspoon of Parmesan cheese and bake until the tops are lightly browned, about 15 to 20 minutes.

Makes 4 servings

POTATO PANCAKES
CHEZ MUSTACHE
AURORA, OREGON

In 1856 Dr. William Keil, a Prussian immigrant arrived in Oregon and set up a communal colony. The members of the colony shared all the work and the rewards that came from that work. It was their attempt at starting a new society and they called their town Aurora. Aurora is the name of the Roman goddess of the dawn, an ancient symbol of a new beginning. The original settlers to this town built a hotel, which soon became famous for its good cooking... especially the potato dishes. Today the famous eatery in town is called Chez Mustache. The chef is Joel Miller and the following recipe is adapted from the Aurora Colony recipe for potato pancakes.

1 **cup mashed potatoes**
1 **egg**
1 1/4 **cups buttermilk**
3/4 **cup flour**
3 **tablespoons minced chives**
Salt and freshly ground black pepper
Vegetable oil to give a 1/4-inch coating to the saute pan

1. In a large bowl, combine the mashed potatoes with the egg until smooth.

2. Add the buttermilk and mix well.

3. Stir in the flour, chives and salt and pepper to taste. You should have a thin pancake batter.

4. Let the batter rest for 10 minutes.

5. In a large skillet, place a small amount of vegetable oil and heat on medium-high. When the oil is hot, drop the batter by 1/4-cup measures into the skillet and fry for about 3 minutes. Turn the pancakes over and cook for 2 to 3 more minutes until browned and cooked through.

Makes approximately 20 pancakes

DRY-FRIED STRING BEANS
SHUN LEE, NEW YORK CITY

For over 20 years the Shun Lee restaurants in New York City have maintained an outstanding reputation for quality. They have taken the best of Chinese cuisine and presented it within an elegant atmosphere. Part of the art of Chinese cooking consists of being able to take a few common ingredients and prepare them in a way that lets each individual flavor element improve all the other ingredients. The following string bean recipe will illustrate the approach.

1 1/2 pounds string beans
1 cup vegetable oil
1 tablespoon chopped scallions
1 teaspoon chopped garlic
1/2 teaspoon Szechuan chili paste or hot sauce
2 tablespoons soy sauce (low-sodium if possible)
1 tablespoon dry sherry or rice wine
1 teaspoon sugar

1. Wash the beans under running water. Dry the beans well on paper towels.

2. In a wok or skillet, heat the oil until just before it smokes. Add the beans, standing back to avoid being spattered with oil. Cook the beans over high heat, stirring and turning frequently, until they are wrinkled and lightly browned, about 7 minutes. Remove the beans with a slotted spoon and place in a colander to drain. Set aside.

3. Discard all but about 2 tablespoons of oil from the skillet. Over high heat, reheat the remaining oil. Add the scallions, garlic and Szechuan paste and stir-fry for 20 seconds. Add the soy sauce and stir.

4. Put the string beans back into the skillet. Add the wine and sugar and stir until well mixed, about one minute. Remove from skillet and serve.

Makes 4 to 6 servings

BAKED APPLE-STUFFED ACORN SQUASH
RITZ HOTEL
PARIS, FRANCE

The Place Vendome in Paris is a center for some of the leading banking institutions of France. It is a place to deposit money and receive dividends. And just below the streets of the Place Vendome is the multi-million dollar health club of The Ritz Hotel, a place to deposit excess body fat and receive tender loving care. This newly constructed club has some amazing facilities. There's a fully equipped exercise room, swimming pool, skin treatment center and a tanning salon. They also have a squash court. The first time someone said squash court to me I thought they were talking about a tribunal where people would judge my squash recipes . . . what did I know?

2 medium acorn squash
2 Golden Delicious apples , or any other baking variety
1/4 cup white wine (or water)
1/4 cup sugar
1/2 teaspoon cinnamon
2 tablespoons butter
4 teaspoons ground almonds

1. Pre-heat the oven to 350 F. Put about 1-inch of water in a baking dish. Set aside.

2. Wash the acorn squash and cut them in half. Scoop out the seeds and slice a thin piece off of the bottom of each half, being careful not to make a hole in the squash. (This slice will give the squash a flat base so it will sit upright in the baking dish.) Place the squash in the baking dish and set aside.

3. Peel and core the apples and cut into thin slices.

4. In a large skillet, combine the wine and the sugar over moderate heat. Add the apples and cook until the apples are crisp-tender and the liquid is slightly reduced, about 2 minutes. Sprinkle the cinnamon on top of the apples, swirl in the butter and continue to cook until the sauce is thick, about 2 to 3 minutes.

5. Place an equal portion of the apple mixture into each of the four squash halves and bake until a knife easily pierces the meat of the squash, about 1 hour. With 10 minutes to cook, sprinkle 1 teaspoon of the almonds on top of the apple mixture.

Makes 4 servings

BUTTERNUT SQUASH AND WINTER PEAR
RITZ HOTEL
PARIS, FRANCE

---

1 **medium butternut squash, about 3 pounds**
2 **Bosc pears, or any other firm variety**
$^1/_3$ **cup slivered almonds**
$^1/_2$ **cup brown sugar**
2 **tablespoons butter or margarine**

1. Pre-heat the oven to 350° F. Butter a baking dish or casserole.

2. Peel the squash, clean out the insides, and cut it into quarters. Slice the quarters into pieces about $^1/_2$ inch thick. Set aside.

3. Peel and core the pears and slice into pieces about the same thickness as the squash.

4. In the casserole dish or baking pan, alternate the squash and the pears. You will have approximately 3 layers of alternating slices. Sprinkle with the almonds, then the brown sugar and finally, dot the top of the casserole with the butter.

5. Bake, uncovered, for approximately 35 minutes, until the squash is tender and cooked through.

Makes 4 servings

DESSERTS, CAKES, TARTS, COOKIES & A PIE

QUICK CHOCOLATE MOUSSE
RITZ HOTEL
PARIS, FRANCE

The Ritz Hotel in Paris, France, has been the favorite hotel for many of the kings of Europe from day one of its operation. A king of considerable importance who unfortunately did not have an opportunity to stay at the Ritz, was Montezuma, ruler of the Aztecs of Mexico during the 16th century. Montezuma believed that the chocolate bean had been brought to earth by the gods. He also believed it was an aphrodisiac and drank about 50 cups of chocolate each day. Without going on record as to the special impact that chocolate may or may not have on one's life in terms of love . . . I would like to say that had Montezuma stayed at the Ritz, I think he would have loved their Chocolate Mousse.

12 ounces bittersweet or semi-sweet chocolate
1 cup heavy cream
4 ounces sweet butter, softened

1. Melt the chocolate in a double boiler. Transfer the chocolate to a large bowl and set aside to cool to room temperature.

2. In a medium bowl, whip the heavy cream until it has soft peaks.

3. Whisk the butter into the room-temperature chocolate until it is well combined. Fold the whipped cream into the chocolate mixture, pour into a serving dish and chill until firm, approximately one hour.

Makes 6 servings

NOTE: This chocolate mousse is best served the day it is made.

ALMOND TILE COOKIES
RITZ-ESCOFFIER COOKING SCHOOL
PARIS, FRANCE

The Ritz Hotel has built what is probably one of the most luxurious cooking schools in the world. The Ritz Escoffier Cooking School attracts amateurs who want to learn to cook as well as professionals who wish to improve their skills. The following two recipes come from the school's pastry class.

2 egg whites
¹/₂ cup sugar
2 ¹/₂ tablespoons flour
²/₃ cup slivered almonds

1. At least 2 hours before baking, mix all of the ingredients in a small mixing bowl until well combined. Cover and refrigerate until ready to bake.

2. Preheat the oven to 400° F. For the best results use a cookie sheet with a non-stick finish. Drop a tablespoon of the batter onto the cookie sheet and gently flatten. Continue until all of the batter is used. Bake 4 to 6 minutes until the edges of the cookies are lightly browned but the centers remain pale in color.

3. Remove the cookies from the oven and immediately lift them off the sheet and drape them over a rolling pin to form a gentle curved shape. Let cool.

Makes about 15 cookies

NOTE: These cookies do not store well. Make them only as you need them and do not make them on a muggy day. (Preparing the batter 24 hours before baking the cookies will improve the results.)

LACY ORANGE COOKIES
RITZ-ESCOFFIER COOKING SCHOOL
PARIS, FRANCE

1/3 cup slivered almonds
1/2 cup sugar
2 1/2 tablespoons flour
Zest of 1 orange, finely grated
3 tablespoons orange juice
3 1/2 tablespoons butter, clarified

1. At least 2 hours before baking, make the batter by combining all of the ingredients in a small bowl. Mix until well blended. Cover and refrigerate until ready to bake.

2. Preheat the oven to 400° F. Line a cookie sheet with parchment paper. Making only 2 to 3 cookies at a time, drop a tablespoon of batter onto the parchment, flatten and bake 3 to 5 minutes until the edges are brown but the center of the cookies remain pale in color. (These cookies will spread a great deal.)

3. Remove the pan from the oven and cool slightly. Pell the cookies off of the paper and place on a rolling pin to form a gently curved cookie. Continue with the remaining batter until all of the cookies are made.

Makes about 16 cookies

NOTE: As with the Almond Tile Cookies, make only as needed because these cookies do not store well. If possible, make the batter 24 hours in advance.

PEACH MELBA
RITZ HOTEL
PARIS, FRANCE

Nellie Melba was a famous singer during the last years of the 1800's. One of her regular roles was in the Wagnerian opera Lohengrin. *A particular scene in this work presents a sculpture of a swan floating across the stage with Miss Melba sitting on top. This part of the opera was much beloved by a distinguished chef of the time by the name of Auguste Escoffier, and it inspired him to create a dessert for the great Nellie. In its original presentation, it consisted of a swan made of ice, supporting peaches and vanilla ice cream, topped with berries. Nellie loved it and ordered it quite often. Eventually it took its toll on poor Nellie's figure, which led Escoffier to develop Melba Toast, as a calorie counterbalance. For many years, Escoffier worked at the Ritz Hotel in Paris. Located in the majestic Place Vendome, it is one of the most sumptuous hotels in the world and as befits an institution of such standing, it has had in residence some of France's leading chefs.*

<u>Raspberry Sauce:</u>
One 10-ounce package frozen raspberries, thawed
2 tablespoons sugar
3 tablespoons raspberry liqueur (optional)

One 16-ounce can sliced peaches, well drained (or fresh pitted peaches if available)
2 pints vanilla ice cream

1. To make the sauce, in a food processor, puree the raspberries and sugar. Add the liqueur and chill or use immediately.

2. In a single serving dish, place a half a peach, cut side up.

3. Top the peach with a scoop of vanilla ice cream and pour some of the raspberry sauce on top. Serve immediately.

Makes 8 servings

WALNUT TART
HALCYON HOTEL
LONDON, ENGLAND

The Holland Park district of London is one of the city's most handsome residential areas, and right in the middle of its tree-lined streets is the small, very beautiful Halcyon Hotel. The Halcyon has become famous for its private home setting, its individually decorated rooms and its excellent restaurant. The restaurant is called The Kingfisher, and it is directed by chef James Robinson, who is responsible for the following tart. Rich and satisfying, a small slice of this delightful pastry makes a perfect ending to a meal.

One 9-inch unbaked pie crust
$^1/_2$ cup unsalted butter
$^1/_2$ cup dark brown sugar
4 egg yolks
$^3/_4$ cup maple syrup
8 ounces walnuts
2 teaspoons freshly squeezed lemon juice
4 teaspoons lemon zest
$^1/_2$ teaspoon vanilla extract
Pinch salt

1. Preheat the oven to 400° F. Line a 9-inch tart pan with the pie crust.

2. In a mixing bowl, cream the butter and brown sugar with an electric mixer until the mixture is smooth and light.

3. With the mixer running, slowly add the egg yolks and maple syrup.

4. Fold in the walnuts, juice, zest, extract and salt. Pour into the tart pan.

5. Set the tart pan on the middle rack of the oven and bake 10 minutes. Reduce heat to 325° F. and bake 30 to 35 minutes longer, or until set.

6. Remove from the oven and let cool before serving.

Makes 8 servings

APPLE PIE
RED ROOF INN ✦ PORTAGE LA PRAIRIE
MANITOBA, CANADA

Clark Gable and Carole Lombard were the great heart-throb film stars of the 1930's and 40's. When Carole fell in love with Clark she consulted with her mother on how to become the apple of Clark's eye. Mama Lombard suggested that Carole develop an interest in one of Gable's hobbies and share it with him. Carole promptly started to take shooting lessons and began to accompany Gable on his duck hunting trips to Canada. They would stay at a little place called the Red Roof Inn at Portage La Prairie in Manitoba. Carole and Clark's favorite room is just as they left it ... same furniture, same bed, the actual dress that Carole would wear to dinner. Carole became the apple of Clark's eye, but the following recipe for the Red Roof Inn's apple pie captured both their hearts.

Never-Fail Pastry (see following recipe)
3 pounds baking apples (about 6 large), peeled, cored and sliced
The juice of 1 lemon
3/4 cup sugar
3 tablespoons flour
1 teaspoon cinnamon
1/4 teaspoon nutmeg
2 tablespoons butter or margarine
1 egg
2 tablespoons sugar

1. Preheat the oven to 425° F. In a large bowl, place the apple slices and sprinkle with the lemon juice. Toss well.

2. Sprinkle the apples with the sugar, flour, cinnamon and nutmeg. Toss well. Set aside.

3. Roll out a portion of the pie dough (about 1/4 if you made the whole recipe) and place in the bottom of a 10-inch pie pan. Press into the pan but do not stretch.

4. Pour the apple filling into the shell and dot with the butter.

5. Roll out another portion of the dough and place on top of the filling. Press the edges together and crimp to keep the filling from spilling out during the cooking.

6. In a small bowl, gently beat the egg. Brush the egg mixture over the crust of the pie, sprinkle with 2 tablespoons of sugar. Cut vents into the pie to allow the steam to escape.

7. Bake at 425° F. for 15 minutes, then reduce the oven temperature to 350° F. and bake for an additional 25 to 30 minutes.

Makes enough filling for one pie, approximately 10 inches in diameter

NEVER-FAIL PASTRY

4 cups all-purpose flour
1 teaspoon baking powder
1 teaspoon salt
1 pound shortening
1 egg
1 tablespoon vinegar
Cold water

1. In a large bowl, mix the flour, baking powder and salt.

2. Cut in the shortening, using a pastry cutter, 2 knifes or the tips of your fingers. The mixture should be the consistency of small peas.

3. In a large measuring cup, place the egg and the vinegar. Then fill the measuring cup to the $3/4$ mark with very cold water.

4. Pour the liquid mixture into the dry ingredients and mix until the dough just pulls together.

5. Wrap and store in the refrigerator if not using immediately.

Makes enough dough for 2 pies, each approximately 10 inches in diameter.

FUDGE CAKE WITH BUTTERCREAM ICING
OPERAKÄLLAREN RESTAURANT
STOCKHOLM, SWEDEN

The Operakällaren Restaurant in Stockholm, Sweden was originally opened in 1787 inside the old Opera House. For over 200 years it has been the Opera's official restaurant. The main dining room was reconstructed in 1895. When it opened it contained a series of paintings with nude people dancing about. The pictures immediately became the subject of great controversy and the artist was called back to add a few more leaves in appropriate places. Today, the Operakällaren is one of the world's great restaurants, famous for their classic Swedish cooking prepared under the direction of Chef Werner Vögeli. Following are two examples of their outstanding desserts.

1 cup flour
1 cup unsweetened cocoa
4 teaspoons baking powder
$^1/_2$ teaspoon salt
4 ounces butter, unsalted
2 cups sugar
4 egg yolks
2 cups milk
2 teaspoons vanilla extract
4 egg whites

1. Preheat oven to 350° F.

2. In a bowl, sift together the flour, cocoa, baking powder and salt.

3. In a second bowl, using an electric mixer, cream the butter and sugar together until the mixture is light and fluffy. When the mixture is fully blended and light, add the egg yolks one at a time and beat for a minute between each yolk.

4. Add the dry ingredients to the butter, sugar and egg yolk mixture, one cup at a time. Pour in some of the milk after each cup of dry ingredients. Add the vanilla extract.

5. Beat the egg whites until they are stiff but not dry. They should be the same consistency as shaving cream. Fold the beaten egg whites into the batter.

6. Pour the batter into three 8-inch cake pans that have been lightly greased and floured.

7. Bake for 30 to 40 minutes, or until the sides of the cakes shrink away from the pan's rims. Cool completely.

8. Spread vanilla buttercream icing in between the layers and over the top and sides. Cover the cake, and store in the refrigerator.

Makes 8 servings

VANILLA BUTTERCREAM ICING

3 ounces unsalted butter, softened
2 teaspoons vanilla extract
$1/8$ teaspoon salt
1 pound confectioners' sugar
$1/4$ cup milk

1. Cream together the butter, vanilla and salt.

2. Gradually beat in the sugar and milk.

3. When the mixture is smooth, place a thin layer between each of the cake layers, and on the sides and top of the cake.

Makes 2 cups

CARROT CAKE WITH CREAM CHEESE ICING
OPERAKÄLLAREN RESTAURANT
STOCKHOLM, SWEDEN

For the Cake:

2 cups sugar
1 1/2 cups vegetable oil
4 eggs, lightly beaten
2 cups all-purpose flour
1 teaspoon salt
2 teaspoons baking soda
2 teaspoons ground cinnamon
1/2 teaspoon grated nutmeg
1/2 teaspoon ground allspice
3 cups finely shredded carrots
  (6 to 8 carrots)
1/2 cup chopped walnuts

For the Icing:

1/2 cup unsalted butter, at room
  temperature
One 8-ounce package cream
  cheese, at room temperature
2 cups confectioners' sugar
2 teaspoons vanilla extract

1. Preheat the oven to 325° F. Butter a 13- x 9- x 2-inch baking pan.

2. In an electric mixer or by hand, thoroughly mix together the sugar, oil and eggs.

3. In a separate bowl, sift together the flour, salt, baking soda and spices. Gradually add the flour mixture to the egg mixture, blending well before adding more.

4. Fold in the carrots and walnuts. Pour the batter into the prepared pan and bake for 1 hour to 1 hour and 10 minutes, or until a wooden toothpick inserted into the center comes out clean. Remove to a rack to cool to room temperature.

5. To make the icing, in a bowl, cream the butter until light and fluffy. Mash the cream cheese with a fork and work it into the butter. Add the confectioners' sugar and vanilla and beat vigorously, until blended.

6. When the cake is cool, spread with the cream cheese icing.

Makes 12 servings

JARLSBERG COFFEE CAKE
GRAND HOTEL
OSLO, NORWAY

The Norwegian landscape is quite striking. Seventy percent of the country is covered with mountains that shoot up into the clouds. Only three percent of the land can be used for farming. The early Norwegians who settled and survived in this environment were good hunters but they were also good thinkers. They realized that every time they had an animal for dinner, they had to go out into those mountains and hunt up another animal for their next dinner. One day, some ancient Norwegian had a great idea . . . keep the animal alive and milk it. Nice beginning, but fresh milk does not last long. The the second great idea came along . . . cheese. Cheese is an ideal way to preserve the nutrients in milk. Third great idea . . . Jarlsberg cheese. Lots of calcium and protein; low in sodium. Fourth great idea . . . Jarlsberg Coffee Cake.

$1/2$ **cup apples, diced**	$1/4$ **cup butter, softened**
$1/2$ **tablespoon fresh lemon juice**	**1 egg, beaten**
$1/2$ **cup sugar**	$1/4$ **cup milk**
$1 1/2$ **cups flour, sifted**	$1/4$ **cup walnuts, chopped**
1 teaspoon baking powder	$1/2$ **cup Jarlsberg cheese, diced**
$1/4$ **teaspoon salt**	$1/2$ **teaspoon cinnamon**
$1/8$ **teaspoon nutmeg**	**1 tablespoon sugar**

1. Preheat the oven to 375° F. Grease an 8- x 8- inch pan.

2. In a small bowl, sprinkle the apples with lemon juice and set aside.

3. In a medium bowl, combine the sugar, flour, baking powder, salt and nutmeg. Stir in the butter and mix well. Add the egg, milk, and nuts. Add the apples and the cheese. Stir to combine.

4. In a small bowl, combine the cinnamon and the tablespoon of sugar.

5. Pour the batter into the prepared pan and sprinkle the cinnamon and sugar on top. Bake for 35 to 40 minutes.

Makes 8 servings

NORWEGIAN HOT APPLE DESSERT
SAS HOTEL
OSLO, NORWAY

The Scandinavian Airline System maintains a group of hotels throughout the world that have continually stressed the importance of their kitchens. This recipe comes from chef Lars Erik Underthun at the SAS Hotel in Oslo, Norway and is quite irresistible.

The juice of 1 lemon
3 large Golden Delicious Apples
1/2 cup water
1/2 cup sugar
1 teaspoon cinnamon
1/2 cup raisins
4 tablespoons butter or margarine

1. Place the lemon juice into a large bowl.

2. Peel, core and slice the apples about 1/2-inch thick and place them in the bowl with the lemon juice. Toss well and set aside.

3. In a large skillet, combine the water, sugar, cinnamon and the raisins. Over high heat, stir this mixture constantly so that the sugar will carmelize without sticking to the pan. This will take approximately 5 to 7 minutes. The mixture will appear caramel in color and thickness.

4. Whisk in the butter and add the apple slices, stirring gently but constantly. The apples will give off some juice and cause the liquid to thin out, after about 6 minutes, the juice will evaporate and the sauce will thicken again.

5. On a dessert plate, place a portion of vanilla sauce (recipe follows) and arrange the apple slices in a fanned-out wheel on top of the sauce. Drizzle a little of the caramel on top of the apples and sprinkle with some of the raisins. Serve warm.

Makes 4 servings

BASIC VANILLA SAUCE

1 cup milk
3 egg yolks
8 tablespoons sugar
1 tablespoon vanilla

1. In a small saucepan over medium heat, bring the milk to a simmer.

2. Meanwhile, in a medium bowl, whisk the eggs and the sugar together until a ribbon forms when the whisk is lifted from the mixture.

3. Whisk constantly while slowly pouring the hot milk into the mixture.

4. Return the mixture to the saucepan. Over low heat, stir constantly with a wooden spoon until the mixture thickens. Be careful not to overcook or the eggs will scramble.

5. The sauce is finished when you can dip a spoon into the sauce, then draw your finger over the back of the spoon and have a track remain that is almost free of sauce.

6. Remove from the heat and stir in the vanilla. Serve or chill and use later.

Makes one cup

CURRANT TART
OSLO, NORWAY

Oslo is the capital city of Norway and one of the most attractive cities in Europe. Tourists are treated to the national attractions and culture, city life, and nature all within the same day. Akerhus Castle and Fortress offer a historical glimpse of the nation. There is a Norwegian Folk Museum with ancient buildings from different time periods and different parts of the country. There is a museum for the 1,000 year old Viking Ships and another for the boat that took Norwegian explorers to the North and South Poles. Oslo also has a magnificent waterfront with stores and restaurants that kept calling me back to the seaside. Of particular interest to me was a small combination bakery and coffee shop that served excellent pastries. The following recipe was adapted from their kitchen.

1 **cup dried currants**
1/4 **cup dark rum**
Pastry for an 11-inch, single-crust tart
4 **tablespoons butter, softened**
1 **cup dark brown sugar**
1/2 **cup light corn syrup**
3 **eggs, lightly beaten**
1 **teaspoon vanilla extract**

1. Preheat the oven to 450° F.

2. In a small bowl, combine the currants and rum and set aside.

3. Roll out the pastry and fit it into an 11-inch tart pan. Prick it all over with a fork. Cover the pastry with aluminum foil and weigh the foil down with dry beans or with aluminum pastry weights.

4. Bake for 5 minutes, remove the foil and beans, re-prick the pastry and bake another 3 to 4 minutes, until the pastry is done. Remove from the oven and lower the temperature to 375° F.

5. In a small bowl, cream the butter and sugar together. Stir in the syrup and eggs. Add the vanilla and the currants and rum.

6. Pour the mixture into the prepared pastry shell. Bake for 35 to 40 minutes, until the top is well browned and the filling firm.

7. Cool to room temperature before serving. Serve with whipped cream.

Makes 12 servings

THE DIFFERENCE BETWEEN A PIE AND A TART
The difference between a pie and a tart is that a pie is generally made with a crust on the top as well as on the bottom, while a tart has only a bottom crust. In France, pies are always made with the crust on the bottom and always called tarts. But in England, a pie is anything baked in a baking dish with a crust on top. They don't always use a crust on the bottom. Shepherd's pie is crusted with mashed potatoes. A pork pie is meat and gravy wrapped in pastry dough and baked. It is called a turnover in America. Pies in fourteenth-century England were called coffins because they were baked in long rectangular tins rather than round pie pans.

An English tart has a pastry crust on the bottom with a fruit filling on top. Anything baked in a pie pan is called a pie in America; pumpkin and pecan pies, among others, do not have top crusts but they are still called pies. The term tart is used to describe a miniature pie.

BREADS, PIZZA, PANCAKES, MARMALADE, JAM, A SEASONING AND TWO BEVERAGES

SASKATCHEWAN WHEAT
THE BEGINNINGS OF CIVILIZATION

Historians tell us that when the last great glaciers began to retreat about 12,000 B.C., the climate began to warm up and fields of wild wheat appeared. This easily available food was collected by our ancestors and soon became an important part of their diet. The gathering tribes had to be on the spot when the grain was ready for harvest, and soon, small settlements grew up at the edges of the wheat fields. Over the next 4,000 years, the gatherers learned to control and cultivate the wild wheat into what became our fist agricultural crop. We learned to separate the edible part of the grain from the surrounding husks, and to germinate or cook the wheat until it was edible. That was quite a sophisticated bit of work—and very important, since raw wheat is difficult to swallow and indigestible.

Wheat products became an essential part of the diet for many of our earliest cultures. Wheat was the basis of the porridges that sustained life for thousands of years. It evolved into bread which is still described as the staff of life.

The Canadian province of Saskatchewan is known as Canada's bread basket because of its enormous production of wheat. The fields owe their rich soil to the glaciers that once covered them. When you look at a wheat field, you are looking at the very beginning of agricultural civilization.

115

BUTTERMILK BANNOCK
GRASS RIVER LODGE
REED LAKE, WINNIPEG, CANADA

The word "bannock" was originally used to describe a barley pancake that has been popular in Scotland for centuries. During the 1700's, it was brought to Canada and the American Colonies by explorers and pioneers. Sometimes the dough is baked to produce a biscuit, other cooks prefer to fry it like a doughnut.

2 1/2 **cups flour**
1 1/2 **teaspoons baking powder**
1/2 **teaspoon salt**
1/4 **teaspoon baking soda**
1 1/3 **cups buttermilk**
Oil for frying

1. In a medium bowl, combine the flour, baking powder, salt and baking soda.

2. Stir in the buttermilk to form a soft, but not sticky dough.

3. Turn the dough out onto a floured surface and knead several times.

4. Roll the dough out to about 1/2-inch thickness and cut out rounds about 3-inches in diameter.

5. Into a large skillet, pour vegetable oil to a depth of 1-inch and heat over a medium-high flame.

6. When the temperature of the oil is about 375° F. (just before the point at which the oil begins to smoke), cook the rounds 2 to 3 minutes per side, until golden. Drain on paper towels. Serve immediately.

Makes about 20 rounds

OREGON OATS AND BUTTERMILK PANCAKES
HEATHMAN HOTEL
PORTLAND, OREGON

The Heathman Hotel in Portland, Oregon has become famous for its excellent breakfasts. A regular feature of their menu are the following pancakes. They are quite filling, low in fat and high in fiber.

1 cup all-purpose flour
3/4 cup buckwheat flour
1 tablespoon baking powder
1 teaspoon salt
3/4 cup oatmeal (not instant) soaked in 1/2 cup skim milk for at least 10 minutes
2 1/4 cups buttermilk
1 egg

1. In a large bowl, combine all of the dry ingredients and the oats and the milk in which they have been soaked.

2. Add the buttermilk and the egg until well combined.

3. Pour the liquid ingredients into the dry ingredients and stir until just combined.

4. On a griddle or in a large skillet, place a small amount of butter or margarine for frying and heat until hot.

5. Drop the pancake batter by 1/4 cup measures onto the hot surface and cook on each side for approximately 1 to 2 minutes. Tiny bubbles on the top surface of the pancakes tell you that the pancakes are ready to be turned over. Serve immediately.

Makes 15 to 20 pancakes

JARLSBERG TWIST BREAD
GRAND HOTEL
OSLO, NORWAY

Count Gustav Wilhelm Jarlsberg of Norway lived from 1641 to 1717. He lived on a fabulous farm near Oslo and his descendents still live on the property.

It counts to be a Count, especially when your name is on a world famous cheese. Jarlsberg is literally the national cheese of Norway and it's used in hundreds of recipes. On my recent visit to Norway the chef at Oslo's Grand Hotel taught me a bread recipe that had a nice twist to it.

1 package dry yeast
1 tablespoon sugar
1 cup water, divided as follows
4 cups flour
1 teaspoon salt
1/3 cup milk
1/4 cup butter, melted
1 egg
3 cups Jarlsberg cheese, shredded (about 1 pound)
2/3 cup parsley

1. In a small bowl, proof the yeast as follows: Place the yeast and sugar in a bowl and add 1/2 cup warm water. The water should not be hot, the ideal temperature is between 110° and 115° F., about the temperature of a baby's formula. Stir to mix and set aside.

2. In a large bowl, combine the flour and the salt. Set aside.

3. In a small saucepan over medium-low heat, combine the milk, melted butter and the remaining 1/2 cup water. Heat to lukewarm.

4. Pour the yeast mixture into the dry ingredients and gently mix. Add the lukewarm milk mixture and the egg and 1 cup of the cheese and mix thoroughly until the dough pulls together into a ball.

5. Turn the dough out onto a floured surface and knead until the dough becomes smooth and elastic, approximately 5 or 6 minutes. Cover and let rise until doubled, about 45 minutes.

6. Punch down the dough and divide in half. Roll out two rectangles of dough approximately 12 x 15-inches and sprinkle each with ¹/₂ of the parsley and the cheese.

7. Beginning at the short end of the rectangle, roll the dough up into a very tight roll, smoothing it out as you go. Slice them, lengthwise, but stop about one inch from one end, as below:

Twist each slice around the other to make a braided loaf and smooth the ends out. Place on a cookie sheet and let rise until double, approximately 30 minutes.

8. Preheat the oven to 400° F. Place the cookie sheet in the oven and bake for 18 to 22 minutes. Immediately remove to a rack to cool.

Makes 2 large loaves

NOTE: The trick to knowing if a loaf of bread is done is simple: turn the bread on its side and tap the bottom. If it is cooked, the sound will be hollow.

GRAND HOTEL

OSLO NORWAY

TORTILLA PIZZAS
AMADEUS RESTAURANT
OLD SAN JUAN, PUERTO RICO

This recipe was developed at the Amadeus Restaurant in Old San Juan, Puerto Rico. It illustrates the most recent influence on the 2,000 year old history of Puerto Rican cookery. First came the Taino Indians, then the Spanish, the West Africans and finally the Americans who arrived during the Spanish American War of 1898. For other recipes from the Amadeus Restaurant, see pages 6, 20 and 21.

1 small onion, chopped
4 cloves of garlic, minced
1 teaspoon butter
4 corn or flour tortillas
2 small tomatoes, chopped
4 teaspoons prepared salsa
4 ounces Monterey Jack cheese, grated
4 ounces Chorizo sausage, sliced thinly
$1/2$ cup sliced black olives
Shredded lettuce for serving

1. In a small skillet, saute the onions and garlic in the butter. Set aside.

2. Preheat the oven to 350° F. Place the 4 tortillas on a large cookie sheet.

3. On each of the tortillas place the ingredients in the following order: a portion of the sauteed onion and garlic mixture, some chopped tomatoes, a teaspoon of salsa, 1 ounce of the cheese, 1 ounce of the sausage, and the black olives.

4. Place the cookie sheet in the oven and bake until the cheese melts and the sausage is heated through. Serve immediately.

Makes 4 individual servings

NOTE: For presentation, place each tortilla in the middle of a large dinner plate and surround it with lots of shredded lettuce.

NORWEGIAN FLATBREAD
MAIHAUGEN FOLK MUSEUM
LILLEHAMMER, NORWAY

The Maihaugen Folk Museum consists of a series of buildings that reproduce the life styles of people who lived in the countryside of Norway in the 1700's. During my visit to the facility, I was taught to prepare flatbread by the traditional method. The following recipe is adapted from that ancient ritual.

1 1/4 pounds white flour
10 ounces rye flour (or whole wheat)
1 teaspoon salt
1/2 teaspoon baking powder
2 1/2 cups warm water

1. In a large bowl, combine all of the ingredients and mix to a bread dough consistency.

2. Place on a generously floured board or countertop and knead several times to smooth out the dough.

3. Roll the dough out to a thickness of 1/2 inch and, using a small bowl as a guide, cut out circles approximately 4 inches in diameter. (Do not stack these circles because the dough will stick together.)

4. Roll out the circles until they are very thin, about 1/8 inch and almost transparent.

5. In a large, ungreased skillet (preferably non-stick) that has been heated to very hot, place the circles, one at a time. Cook each circle about 2 minutes on each side, until the bread becomes crisp. Pop any air bubbles that may form on the surface of the bread with a small knife.

Makes 20 to 22 flatbreads

SPICED BLUEBERRY JAM
THE OWL'S NEST
PANGMAN, SASKATCHEWAN, CANADA

Just north of Montana, across the Canadian border is an area known as the Badlands. It was the hide-out for Butch Cassidy and the Sundance Kid, as well as, a considerable number of other devilish desperados. The land might be bad but the cooking is pretty good. Candice and Peter Sotropa run a charming guest house called The Owl's Nest. It is located just outside of Pangman, Saskatchewan. Candice is well known for her pies and preserves which are made from the local berries. The following two recipes were adapted from her kitchen.

One 12 ounce package of frozen blueberries, thawed, room temperature, and crushed
$^1/_2$ cup water
$^1/_4$ teaspoon almond flavoring
$^1/_4$ teaspoon cinnamon
2 tablespoons orange juice concentrate, thawed
7 teaspoons Sure-Jell fruit pectin ($^1/_2$ of a 1 $^3/_4$-ounce box)
2 cups sugar

1. In a medium saucepan, mix the blueberries, water, almond flavoring, cinnamon, and orange juice. Add the Sure-Jell pectin and bring to full rolling boil over high heat, stirring constantly. Add the sugar and continue boiling for 1 minute, stirring constantly.

2. Remove from the heat and skim off and discard any foam with a metal spoon. When cool, pour into containers to 1/2-inch from the tops of the containers. Cover. Store in the refrigerator for up to 3 weeks.

Makes 3 cups

HONEY, CRANBERRY, ORANGE MARMALADE
THE OWL'S NEST
PANGMAN, SASKATCHEWAN, CANADA

2 cups honey
3 cups fresh or frozen cranberries
6 oranges, peeled and grated in the food processor

1. In a medium saucepan, heat the honey until liquid and smooth over medium heat. Add the cranberries and cook for 10 minutes. Stir in the oranges. Bring to a boil and cook for 3 minutes, stirring constantly.

2. Remove from heat and cool. Pour into containers and store in the refrigerator for up to 3 weeks.

Makes 4 cups.

ABOUT CRANBERRIES
Cranberries are tart red berries and were harvested in the bogs of eastern Massachusetts and Cape Cod by the Pequot and Narraganset Indians long before the colonists touched land at Provincetown.

The Dutch gave cranberries their name after the word *kranbeere*. Commercial cultivation of cranberries began on Cape Cod in 1816. New Jersey, Wisconsin and Oregon are also major producers. Cranberries are harvested between Labor Day and Halloween, and although there is no proof, the Indians probably brought cranberries to the first Thanksgiving.

Nutritionally, cranberries are a very good source of vitamin C and fiber. They are low in calories, but because they are commonly cooked in sugar to compensate for their tart nature, most preparations end up fairly high in calories.

HOT CHOCOLATE
HOLMENKOLLEN SKI MUSEUM
OSLO, NORWAY

The Holmenkollen Ski Museum in Oslo, Norway, originally opened in 1923, and is totally devoted to the history of skiing. From the 4,000 year old rock carving that shows an ancient skier (see below) to the story of Telemark, this building tours you through the trails and tales. Experts tell me that the selection of the proper equipment for skiing is of critical importance. My personal contribution to the paraphernalia is my favorite recipe for hot chocolate . . . I have my own priorities.

1 **rounded teaspoon cocoa**
2 **rounded teaspoons sugar (or modify to taste)**
1 **cup milk**

1. In a small saucepan, combine the cocoa, sugar and 1 tablespoon of milk. Stir over a low heat until you have a smooth paste.

2. Slowly add the remaining milk and continue stirring and heating, but do not allow mixture to boil.

3. Just before serving, use a whisk to beat a foam on the top of the chocolate. Pour the chocolate into a serving cup, allowing the foam to float on top.

NOTE: A pinch of cinnamon, nutmeg, or a few drops of vanilla can be added as additional flavorings. The above recipe can be increased for as many servings as desired, keeping the same proportions.

Makes 1 serving

PIÑA COLADA
LE LO LAI FESTIVAL
SAN JUAN, PUERTO RICO

1 ounce cream of coconut
4 ounces freshly squeezed unsweetened pineapple juice
$^1/_2$ cup ice
2 ounces light or gold rum
Pineapple slice, for garnish

1. Combine all ingredients except the pineapple slice in a blender container and blend for 10 to 20 seconds. Pour into a cocktail glass and garnish with a pineapple slice.

Makes 1 serving

HOW TO MAKE COCONUT MILK OR CREAM
The liquid that comes out of a fresh whole coconut is called coconut milk, but there is another version that is used in cooking. This variety—culinary coconut milk or cream—is made by pouring hot water on grated fresh coconut. The mixture is left to steep for 10 minutes and then is poured through a double layer of cheesecloth and squeezed. The liquid that comes out is coconut milk or cream.

Another method is to place the coconut meat in an electric blender with water and blend for 10 seconds. Again strain through cheesecloth.

Coconut milk is as perishable as fresh cow's milk. It should be kept in a closed container in the refrigerator and used within 3 to 4 days.

It is possible to use coconut milk as a drink, but it is not a real substitute for cow's milk since it doesn't have the same protein or nutritional benefits.

Coconut milk will curdle if cooked at a high heat. It is best to add it to dishes at the very last minute, or use a double boiler.

SOFRITO
LUQUILLO KIOSKOS, PUERTO RICO

Sitting on the northeast coast of Puerto Rico is the El Yunque rain forest. It is the only rain forest in the U.S. National Park Service and it collects over 100 billion gallons of rain each year. At the foot of the forest is Luquillo Beach, one of the most beautiful beaches in the Caribbean and a favorite spot for the residents of San Juan. It is what separates the forest from the beach that is of great interest to me. The median between these two natural wonders is a man-made surprise, Los Kioskos. A row of 60 little fast food restaurants specializing in seafood, and to a gringo like myself, other unidentified frying objects. The key ingredient in many of their dishes is Sofrito, an aromatic sauce made from pureed tomatoes, onions, garlic, peppers and spices. Almost every cook in Puerto Rico has some Sofrito on hand to flavor whatever else they are cooking.

1 cup vegetable oil
6 ounces prosciutto or lean cured ham, cut into 1/4-inch pieces
2 medium onions, chopped
2 large green bell peppers, seeded, ribs removed, chopped
4 red Italian frying peppers, or 2 medium red bell peppers, seeded, ribs removed, chopped
6 cloves garlic, chopped
20 fresh cilantro leaves, chopped
4 teaspoons dried oregano

1. In a large stockpot, heat the oil. Add the prosciutto and saute until golden over medium heat. Reduce the heat to low and add the remaining ingredients. Simmer about 10 minutes or until tender, stirring occasionally.

2. Cool thoroughly and spoon into freezer containers, filling 3/4 full. Freeze. Transfer as needed to the refrigerator. A few tablespoons of this mixture is often added as seasoning to a Puerto Rican recipe.

Makes 5 cups

FOLKLORE

A BRIEF HISTORY OF TABLE SERVICE
FROM A LA FRANCAISE TO A LA RUSSE
THE RITZ HOTEL ♦ PARIS, FRANCE

Starting in the middle ages and for hundreds of years thereafter, when a serious dinner was served, it was presented in a fashion called *a la francaise*, which means "the French style." It consisted of many different dishes all displayed at the same time.

The actual dishes on the table might be changed three or four times, but each display included meat, fish, poultry, vegetables and sweets. The objective was to have as impressive a presentation as possible ... the more the better ... and all at once. During the second half of the 1800's a new fashion arrived called *a la russe*, which means "the Russian style."

A la russe is the system we use today, with one course following the other in a more or less predetermined pattern of appetizer, soup, main course and dessert. The Russian method had two great advantages. First, the food could be presented when it was ready to eat and second, waste was greatly reduced.

Two of the great promoters of the new service were August Escoffier and Cesar Ritz. They had teamed up at the Ritz Hotel in Paris in 1896. Escoffier was the chef and he liked this system because his food tasted better. Ritz ran the hotel. He enjoyed the quality, of course, but this new method also gave him some control over the estimated quantities. Ritz could always have at hand what his guests desired. One hundred years have gone by and the Ritz Hotel still has the same approach ... what you want, when you want it.

PONCE DE LEON AND THE DIET OF YOUTH

Ponce de Leon was a Spanish explorer who traveled with Christopher Columbus, and became extremely important to Puerto Rico. Ponce found gold on the island in 1508, and decided to move in and set up shop. More than anyone else, he was responsible for the early Spanish colonization of the Puerto Rican community. Walk through the streets of the city of old San Juan and you will see his influence. The Whitehouse, built as Ponce de Leon's residence, still stands, as do many of the buildings originally constructed during the early days of European colonization of Puerto Rico.

Ponce de Leon undertook a series of exploratory voyages from the island. He was the first European to see what is now the United States when he discovered Florida. Historians say that Ponce was looking for the fountain of youth, a spring that would supply him with perpetual boyhood. He never found it, but these days scientists are making a good case for a diet that can help preserve your good health. The key elements are low fat, low cholesterol, low sodium and lots of complex carbohydrates. Not as simple as just sipping the fountain of youth . . . but who said it was going to be easy?

NORWEGIAN FOOD TRADITIONS
MAIHAUGEN MUSEUM
LILLEHAMMER, NORWAY

Maihaugen is an amazing open-air museum near the Norwegian city of Lillehammer. It is made up of a group of buildings that were actually constructed in the mid-1700's. They formed a working farm community, and are being preserved as a museum of what life was like over 200 years ago. It reminds me of how very much Norway's weather patterns influence the traditional cooking of the country.

Norway has a very short growing season and a very long winter, and that has had an enormous impact on the food of the country. Until the introduction of 20th-Century food technology, everything that was harvested at the end of the short summer had to be preserved through the long winter.

When you look at the favorite foods of the Norwegian people you can see their ancient reliance on foods that last. *Gravlax* is salmon that has been preserved by salting. Smoked salmon has been preserved by the action of the smoke. Herring has been preserved by brine solutions, wine or vinegar. Cheese is actually a way of preserving the nutrients in fresh milk. Norway's most traditional breads are made without yeast . . . dry and crisp and able to last for months and months without the loss of taste or nutrition. Even the sardine is a Norwegian approach to preserving a small local fish called a Brisling

RUM BREAK

The Thames River in London is home to the British Navy and its centuries of tradition and history. After the destruction of the Spanish Armada in 1588, English warships ruled the waves. It was during this time that a British Admiral introduced the rum break, similar to a coffee break, but the beverage is one part rum to three parts water. The drink was called grog, which was the nickname of the Admiral who introduced the idea. Since then, rum has been mixed with fruit juice, tomato juice, tonic, soda and just about anything else that was at hand. Admiral Grog's rum break stayed as part of British Naval tradition right into the 1970's.

The Spanish were master rum producers and thought rum was an elegant drink. During the 1800's, Pedro Fernandez, an engineer for the Spanish government in Puerto Rico, began making a rum for his family that was so smooth that no one mixed it with anything. They drank it by itself, like a Cognac. The secret technique for its production appears to involve the addition of tiny amounts of macerated fruit and many years of aging in the barrel. As a matter of fact, the bottles that are available to the public each year are marked Ron del Barrilito, which translates as Rum from the barrel.